The Wisdom of
JANE AUSTEN

The Wisdom of

JANE AUSTEN

EDITED BY
SHAWNA MULLEN

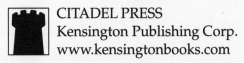

CITADEL PRESS
Kensington Publishing Corp.
www.kensingtonbooks.com

Kensington Publishing Corp.
850 Third Avenue
New York, NY 10022

All Kensington titles, imprints, and distributed lines are available at special quantity discounts for bulk purchases for sales promotions, premiums, fund-raising, educational, or institutional use. Special book excerpts or customized printings can also be created to fit specific needs. For details, write or phone the office of the Kensington special sales manager: Kensington Publishing Corp., 850 Third Avenue, New York, NY 10022, attn: Special Sales Department, phone: 1-800-221-2647.

CITADEL PRESS and the Citadel logo are Reg. U.S. Pat. & TM Off.

First printing: June 2003

10 9 8 7 6 5 4 3 2 1

Printed in the United States of America

Library of Congress Control Number: 2002116658

ISBN 0-8065-2507-X

For Isabelle and Jay

Where shall I begin? Which of all my important nothings shall I tell you first?

—*Letters of Jane Austen*

CONTENTS

FOREWORD:
THE WORLD OF JANE AUSTEN

Jane Austen's characters have captured hearts and minds for more than 150 years. Courageous, spirited, and charming, her heroines know how to wield the power of a glance. We trust that Jane knew, too—although only a single portrait of her survives—and her letters show proof that the power of her lively and witty prose came from a lively and witty personality.

Unfortunately, what is truly known about Jane Austen amounts to just a glimpse: Aside from her novels and some stories, only 150 letters and a few reports from friends and relatives survive. She lived a short and seemingly quiet life, mostly in the English countryside—but her imagination took in (and brings to us still) a wide and richly imagined world.

Steventon Rectory

Born on December 16, 1775, to George Austen, a parish rector, and Cassandra Leigh Austen, Jane Austen was the sixth in a family of eight children. She grew up at Steventon, a small country parsonage near Basingstoke, Hampshire. The house was "roomy and commodious" by Jane's own account, and very pleasantly situated with a walled garden, strawberry beds, and an adjoining wooded walk. Enfolded by forested hills, and surrounded by farms with winding lanes and scattered cottages, the views on every side must have been charming.

Jane's family were lesser gentry, never really financially

secure, but well educated and somewhat well connected. Her father had a fine intellect and received a wonderful education. Awarded a scholarship to St. John's at Oxford, George Austen went on to become a Fellow of his college, and later a clergyman. He taught student boarders at Steventon Rectory, and was rector of two village parishes, Steventon and Deane. Although there are no accounts that he set out to educate his daughters (they attended schools in their turn), it's likely he directed their studies. Likely, too, that an atmosphere of learning prevailed at home, where George Austen's fine library of more than 500 volumes was freely shared with Jane and her siblings.

Cassandra Leigh Austen, Jane's mother, was also no stranger to schools and learning, for her father taught at Oxford and her uncle was the master of Balliol College. In fact, it is probably through her connection to Oxford that she and her husband met. She came from a slightly wealthier family background than George Austen did, one whose ancestors included nobility. By all accounts, she is said to have been clever and good at poetry and light verse. It comes down to us that she was anxious about her unmarried daughters, but given the near certain fate of genteel poverty for unmarried women (of the Austens' class), how could she not have been—as Jane's own character Mrs. Bennet of *Pride and Prejudice* might be quick to point out.

Early Influences

With five brothers (one brother was ill from birth and never lived at home) and a sister, Jane must have been shaped as much by siblings as she was by her parents' love of reading and books. She was most attached to her older (by two years) sister, Cassandra—their close relationship is famously detailed in one of their mother's letters: "If Cassandra were going to have her head cut off, Jane would insist on sharing her fate."

Cassandra notwithstanding, five brothers had their own influence on "Jenny,"as Jane was called at home. James, the oldest and ten years Jane's elder, loved reading and literature and shared this passion with his sister. He was later to write a memoir about Jane, published in 1870. Edward had a fun-loving and amusing spirit, and his absence must have been felt keenly when he was adopted as a small boy. Distant cousins of the Austens, a wealthy, childless couple named Knight, persuaded his parents to allow them to raise Edward. As an adult, Edward inherited the considerable Knight fortune and estates, and was able to house his elderly mother, Jane, and Cassandra very comfortably.

Henry, good-humored and reportedly Jane's favorite brother, had a colorful career that spanned the militia, banking (and bankruptcy), and the church. Just three years older than Jane, Henry played another great role besides that of beloved brother: For several years of his life he lived in London, and thus was able to be Jane's liaison to her publisher. He saw the novels *Persuasion* and *Northanger Abbey* through to publication after her death.

Two younger brothers, Francis and Charles, were the family's adventurers. Both joined the British Navy and rose successfully in the ranks. Francis became senior admiral of the Fleet, while Charles served as a rear admiral, and later commander in chief of East India Station. Although Jane claimed imagination, rather than real people, as the inspiration for her characters, it is likely that William Price of *Mansfield Park*, and Admiral Croft and Captain Wentworth of *Persuasion*, gathered some of their seamanship from Francis and Charles. However they came by it, it is sure that Jane was devoted to her brothers, faithfully corresponding with them in whatever distant station they visited.

He knows nothing of his own destination, he says, but desires me to write directly, as the 'Endymion' will probably sail in three or four days. He will receive my yesterday's letter, and I shall write again by this post to thank

and reproach him. We shall be unbearably fine. (From a
letter to Cassandra, regarding Charles)

Her devotion perhaps even shows a bit in her work, for a certain thread of fascination (and delight) with ships, sailors,
and the British Navy runs through several of her books.

Away at School

Any seagoing savvy aside, women in Jane Austen's era
were given little formal education. At the ages of seven and
nine, Jane and her sister were briefly taught by a widow
who ran a school at Oxford. When a serious illness (diph-
theria, as the theory goes) ran through the school, they
returned home and remained there for a year. Next, they attended the Abbey School, along with their cousin Emily
Cooper. Ancient and beautiful, the school building adjoined
the old Abbey of Reading, consecrated by Becket in 1125.

If the Abbey were something of a model for Mrs. God-
dard's boarding school in *Emma*, then its teaching style
might have been that of an "old-fashioned Boarding school,
where a reasonable amount of accomplishments were sold
at a reasonable price, and where girls might . . . scramble
themselves into a little education without any danger of
coming back prodigies." Jane and Cassandra attended for
two years (1785 until the spring of 1787). At age eleven, her
"formal"education complete, Jane returned home to the class-
room of her family life and her father's library.

Beginnings of a Writer

It is fair to assume that Jane came by her love of words and
language very young. Her literary leanings, especially her
love of the English poet Crabbe, inspired a family joke that
she would become Mrs. Crabbe if ever given the chance.

The exact date of her first stories is unknown, but she was amusing her family with her plays, and their wildly improbable plots, by the age of twelve.

The Austens loved theatricals, and in 1787, this love was fueled by a year-long visit from a cousin, Eliza de Feuillide. The married, wealthy, and glamorous Eliza loved to act, and her sophistication and flair made quite an impression on the Austens, especially Jane. Inspired, no doubt, by her cousin's stories of life abroad, Jane invented this exotic pedigree for one of her early heroines:

> My father was a native of Ireland and an inhabitant of Wales; my mother was the natural daughter of a Scotch peer by an Italian Opera girl—I was born in Spain and received my education at a convent in France.

This heroine's irreverent story is told in "Love and Friendship," an amusing and exaggerated tale that Jane dedicated to Eliza. Eliza's life makes quite a theatrical story on its own: Her mother, Philadelphia (George Austen's sister), had traveled out to the colonies of India in search of suitors and fortune. This was so risky and extraordinarily dangerous at the time that it is surprising she was allowed to go. In India, she met and married a member of the English gentry and had a daughter, Eliza. As a young girl, Eliza was sent to be educated in Paris; she there met and married a French aristocrat, the Comte de Feuillide. Eliza lived through the unrest preceding the French Revolution, and she and her young son managed (narrowly) to escape the violence. Unfortunately, the Comte did not, and he was put to death in 1794, during the Reign of Terror. After some time back in England, Eliza married Jane's brother Henry in a match that had something of a scandalous flavor. Years later, during the brief peace of Amiens, she prevailed upon Henry to return with her to France, in hopes of regaining some of her property. The couple barely escaped becoming *detenus,* Buonaparte having ordered all English travelers at that time detained. Eliza's French was so perfect, the story goes, that she was able to pass as a native and to once again escape (with her husband) to England.

The Austens' warm and amused response to Jane's stories must have seemed a great encouragement to the young writer. Her father furthered this encouragement by keeping her supplied with blank copybooks—paper and writing implements not being in plentiful supply in that era. In one such book, he wrote the inscription: "Effusions of Fancy by a very Young Lady Consisting of Tales in a Style Entirely new." The tales recorded in these copybooks (often comically) try on many genres—from verse and drama to histories and romances—as Jane's style gathered strength and found its voice.

During the last five years the Austens lived at Steventon rectory, Jane wrote three enduring works, *Pride and Prejudice, Sense and Sensibility,* and *Northanger Abbey.* Most of this writing was done in the family sitting room—perhaps at a small table, but certainly not with the help of privacy or a private desk. Although her family knew that Jane was a writer, she kept the pursuit from friends and neighbors, often working on small pieces of paper that could be easily concealed in a pocket or beneath needlework, should visitors enter the room. In the late eighteenth century it was unusual for a woman to be a writer, and even more unusual for writing by women to be taken seriously.

First Impressions (later titled *Pride and Prejudice),* written in just ten months and completed when Jane was twenty-one, was the first work to be sent out formally, with the hope it might be published. But this was not to be. The London publisher Cadell refused the manuscript and Jane put the pages away for more than a decade. Two years later, in 1798, *Northanger Abbey* met with better success and was accepted by the publishers Crosbie and Company. Jane was paid ten pounds for her work, but the publication date did not arrive: For reasons unknown, Crosbie kept the manuscript but made no attempt to publish it as a book.

Romance and Relocation

Even the casual reader of Jane Austen knows that to travel through the world of her books is to travel through a world of parties and balls, where flirtations are frequent, and courtship sought after. So what of the real Jane's life? Entertainments, at least, were as numerous as those in her fictions: suitors, what we know of them, seem to have been fewer.

In a 1796 letter to her sister, Cassandra (Jane was twenty-one at the time), she writes:

> Tell Mary that I make over Mr. Heartley and all his estate to her for her sole use and benefit in future, and not only him, but all my other admirers into the bargain wherever she can find them, even the kiss which C. Powlett wanted to give me, as I mean to confine myself in future to Mr. Tom Lefroy, for whom I do not care sixpence. Assure her also, as a last and indisputable proof of Warren's indifference to me, that he actually drew that gentleman's picture for me, and delivered it to me without a sigh.

Tom Lefroy was Jane's age, and an Irish relative of Jane Austen's close older friend, Mrs. Anne Lefroy. The Jane Austen who had once covered her father's parish ledger with the imagined names of husbands, "Henry Frederick Howard Fitzwilliam," "Edmund Arthur William Mortimer," now had, at least if her letter is to believed, found an intriguing real-life possibility. The attraction was mutual, as was the flirtation. Jane wrote to Cassandra of their behavior at a dance: "Imagine to yourself everything most profligate and shocking in the way of dancing and sitting down together." Although Tom Lefroy's relatives disapproved of the flirtation, knowing Jane was too poor to enable them to marry, Jane seemed to confide different expectations to her sister (although she remains ever humorous): "I rather expect to receive an offer from my friend in the course of the evening. I shall refuse him, however, unless he promises to give away his white Coat."

The happy ending she perhaps had imagined was not to be. Tom returned to Ireland, where he eventually rose to the position of chief justice. He married an heiress and produced a large family, but did confess in old age to having loved "the great Jane Austen."

In late 1800, Jane's father, then nearing seventy and in failing health, decided to relocate the family to Bath. All of Jane's brothers had settled away from home by then, and the move to the relatively bustling city of Bath affected only Jane and Cassandra. Although she succeeded in voicing optimism about the prospect of moving at the time, years later she wrote to Cassandra with "what happy feelings of escape" she left Bath.

Whatever her state while there, Jane wrote the unfinished story, now published under the title of "The Watsons," during her time in Bath. Her nephew and biographer, J. E. Austen-Leigh, notes of Jane's Bath years that she "went a good deal into society, in a quiet way, chiefly with ladies; and that her eyes were always open to minute traits of character in those with whom she associated."

Her sallies into Bath society may not have been exclusively devoted to spending time among other ladies. Austen-Leigh relates (if his report is true) one further romantic adventure of his aunt during her stay there:

> There is, however, one passage of romance in her history with which I am imperfectly acquainted, and to which I am unable to assign name, or date, or place, though I have it on sufficient authority. Many years after her death, some circumstances induced her sister Cassandra to break through her habitual reticence, and to speak of it.

She said that, while staying at some seaside place, they became acquainted with a gentleman, whose charm of person, mind, and manners was such that Cassandra thought him worthy to possess and likely to win her sister's love. When they parted, he expressed his intention of soon seeing them again; and Cassandra felt no doubt as to his motives. But they never again met. Within a short time they heard of his sudden death. I believe that, if Jane ever loved, it was this unnamed gentleman; but the acquaintance had been short, and I am unable to say whether her feelings were of such a nature as to affect her happiness.

Of Jane's love life, the only other (surviving) record of any event dates to December 2, 1802. Jane and Cassandra were staying with longtime family friends, the Biggs, at their estate in Manydown. Harris Bigg-Wither, a friend since childhood and six years younger than Jane, proposed. She accepted, perhaps in the shock of the moment, although she confessed to Cassandra later that evening that she did not love him. The next day, Jane thought the better of having accepted, and she and her sister raced to the home of their brother James in nearby Steventon, asking to be taken back to Bath. The whole event must have been socially embarrassing, but neither heart seems to have been seriously affected—as the Austens continued in friendship with Mr. Bigg-Withers through the years that followed.

Notoriously, no letter from Jane to Cassandra survives from this period (June 1801 to August 1804). It is almost certain that her sister removed any evidence of Jane having alluded to these incidents. In the end, neither Jane nor her sister ever married.

Chawton House

In February 1805, George Austen died at Bath, and was buried at Walcot Church. His widow and daughters stayed on for a few months, and then removed to "a commodious oldfashioned house in a corner of Castle Square" in South-ampton. Four years later, in 1809, Jane's brother Edward—now Lord Knight—was able to offer his mother and sisters Chawton House, located near his Godmersham Park estate in Kent. The same year, Jane, her mother, Cassandra, and close family friend Emily Lloyd settled at Chawton Cottage.

Chawton was truly a second home to Jane, Steventon having been the first: In her temporary residences at Bath and Southampton, she subtly gives the impression of hav-ing felt a stranger in a strange land. Chawton is also the place most closely linked with Jane Austen the writer, for it is there that she either wrote or reworked, and prepared for publication, the books that have made her famous.

J. E. Austen-Leigh described the house as follows:

It was so close to the road that the front door opened upon it; while a very narrow enclosure, paled in on each side, protected the building from danger of collision with any runaway vehicle. I believe it had been originally built for an inn, for which purpose it was certainly well situ-ated. Afterwards it had been occupied by Mr Knight's steward; but by some additions to the house, and some judicious planting and screening, it was made a pleasant and commodious abode. Mr Knight was experienced and adroit at such arrangements, and this was a labour of love to him. A good-sized entrance and two sitting-rooms made the length of the house, all intended originally to look upon the road, but the large drawing-room window was blocked up and turned into a book-case, and another opened at the side which gave to view only turf and trees, as a high wooden fence and hornbeam hedge shut out the Winchester road, which skirted the whole length of the little domain. Trees were planted each side to form a shrubbery walk, carried round the enclosure, which gave a sufficient space for ladies' exercise. There was a pleasant irregular mixture of hedgerow, and gravel walk, and orchard, and long grass for mowing, arising from two or three little enclosures having been thrown together. The house itself was quite as good as the generality of parsonage houses then were, and much in the same style; and was capable of receiving other members of the family as frequent visitors. It was sufficiently well furnished; everything inside and out was kept in good repair, and it was altogether a comfortable and ladylike establishment, though the means which supported it were not large.

This was the home where, after just a few years residence, and while only in her forties, Jane Austen began to waste away. The cause of her illness is not known, but is presumed to have been cancer.

While at Chawton, Jane Austen revised *Sense and Sensibility*, which was accepted in 1810–1811 for publication, but with the terms "at her own risk."Credited as a novel "By a Lady,"only Jane Austen's family knew of her authorship.

Jane soon turned to revising *Pride and Prejudice*, which she subsequently sold in November 1812, and saw published in late January 1813. A second edition of *Sense and Sensibility* was printed in the fall of 1813, and *Mansfield Park* was published the following spring.

Jane Austen finished *Persuasion* in the summer of 1816, but she was becoming increasingly unwell. In 1817, she began another work, *Sanditon*, but was unable to finish the work. She died in Winchester on Friday, July 18, 1817, and was buried at Winchester Cathedral on July 24.

Her novels *Persuasion* and *Northanger Abbey* were readied for publication by Henry, and published after her death, in the winter of 1817. Although both were credited as having been "written by the author of *Pride and Prejudice* and *Mansfield Park*," Henry added a biographical note identifying Jane Austen, for the first time, as the author.

KEY TO ABBREVIATIONS

The quotes cited in this collection are selections from Jane Austen's novels and letters. Following each quotation is an abbreviation indicating its source. Further publication details may be found in the bibliography.

EM	*Emma*
JAL	*Jane Austen's Letters*
JU	*Juvenilia*
LF	*Love and Friendship*
LS	*Lady Susan*
MP	*Mansfield Park*
NA	*Northanger Abbey*
PER	*Persuasion*
PP	*Pride and Prejudice*
SS	*Sense and Sensibility*

The Wisdom of
JANE AUSTEN

Accomplishment

"No one can be really esteemed accomplished, who does not greatly surpass what is usually met with. A woman must have a thorough knowledge of music, singing, drawing, dancing, and the modern languages, to deserve the word; and besides all this, she must possess a certain something in her air and manner of walking, the tone of her voice, her address and expressions, or the word will be but half deserved."
Caroline Bingley, PP

So far her improvement was sufficient—and in many other points she came on exceedingly well; for though she could not write sonnets, she brought herself to read them; and though there seemed no chance of her throwing a whole party into raptures by a prelude on the pianoforte, of her own composition, she could listen to other people's performance with very little fatigue. Her greatest deficiency was in the pencil—she had no notion of drawing—not enough even to attempt a sketch of her lover's profile, that she might be detected in the design. There she fell miserably short of the true heroic height. At present she did not know her own poverty, for she had no lover to portray.
NA

"It is amazing to me," said Bingley, "how young ladies can have patience to be so very accomplished as they all are."

"All young ladies accomplished! My dear Charles, what do you mean?"

"Yes all of them, I think. They all paint tables, cover skreens, and net purses. I scarcely know any one who cannot do all this, and I am sure I never heard a young lady spoken of for the first time, without being informed that she was very accomplished."

"Your list of the common extent of accomplishments," said Darcy, "has too much truth. The word is applied to many a woman who deserves it no otherwise than by netting a purse, or covering a skreen.
Charles Bingley, Fitzwilliam Darcy, PP

Acting

"It is as a dream, a pleasant dream!" he exclaimed, breaking forth again, after a few minutes' musing. "I shall always look back on our theatricals with exquisite pleasure. There was such an interest, such an animation, such a spirit diffused. Everybody felt it. We were all alive. There was employment, hope, solicitude, bustle, for every hour of the day. Always some little objection, some little doubt, some little anxiety to be got over. I never was happier."
Henry Crawford, MP

Adolescents

I shall think with tenderness and delight on [my young nephew's] beautiful and smiling countenance and interesting manner, until a few years have turned him into an ungovernable, ungracious fellow.
JAL

Advice

It was, perhaps, one of those cases in which advice is good or bad only as the event decides.
PER

Let her think & act as she chuses, however. I have never yet found that the advice of a Sister could prevent a young Man's being in love if he chose it.
LS

Affectation

"I suspect," said Elinor, "that to avoid one kind of affectation, Edward here falls into another. Because he believes many people pretend to more admiration of the beauties of Nature than they really feel, and is disgusted with such pretensions, he affects greater indifference and less discrimination in viewing them himself than he possesses. He is fastidious and will have an affectation of his own."
Elinor Dashwood, SS

Affection

Edmund had been her champion and her friend: he had supported her cause or explained her meaning, he had told her not to cry, or had given her some proof of affection which made her tears delightful . . .
MP

Affluence

"It is a melancholy consideration. Born to the prospect of such affluence! I cannot conceive a situation more deplorable. The interest of two thousand pounds—how can a man live on it? . . . I cannot picture to myself a more wretched condition."
John Dashwood, SS

Age

"Mine is an active, busy mind, with a great many independent resources; and I do not perceive why I should be more in want of employment at forty or fifty than one-and-twenty."
Emma Woodhouse, EM

But seven years, I suppose, are enough to change every pore of one's skin and every feeling of one's mind.
JAL

By the bye, as I must leave off being young, I find many Douceurs in being a sort of chaperon [at dances], for I am put on the Sofa near the Fire & can drink as much wine as I like.
JAL

I am much obliged to you for writing to me again so soon; your letter yesterday was quite an unexpected pleasure. Poor Mrs. Stent! it has been her lot to be always in the way; but we must be merciful, for perhaps in time we may come to be Mrs. Stents ourselves, unequal to anything, and unwelcome to everybody.
JAL

"The older a person grows, Harriet, the more important it is that their manners should not be bad; the more glaring and disgusting any loudness, or coarseness, or awkwardness becomes. What is passable in youth is detestable in later age."
Emma Woodhouse, EM

It sometimes happens that a woman is handsomer at twenty-nine than she was ten years before; and, generally speaking, if there has been neither ill health nor anxiety, it is a time of life at which scarcely any charm is lost.
PER

Mrs. Bates, the widow of a former vicar of Highbury, was a very old lady, almost past every thing but tea and quadrille.
EM

Middle age

Surely that time is now at hand. You are this day 55. If a woman may ever be said to be in safety from the determined Perseverance of disagreeable Lovers and the cruel Persecutions of obstinate Fathers, surely it must be at such a time of Life.
LF

Ambiguity

It appeared to her that he did not excel in giving those clearer insights, in making those things plain which he had before made ambiguous.
NA

Ambition

"That is what I like; that is what a young man ought to be. Whatever be his pursuits, his eagerness in them should know no moderation, and leave him no sense of fatigue."
Marianne Dashwood, SS

"I must look down upon anything contented with obscurity when it might rise to distinction."
Mary Crawford, MP

Amiability

"No, Emma; your amiable young man can be amiable only in French, not in English. He may be very 'amiable,' have very good manners, and be very agreeable; but he can have no English delicacy towards the feelings of other people— nothing really amiable about him."
John Knightley, EM

Various as were the tempers in her father's house, he pleased them all. He endured too well, stood too well with every body. He had spoken to her with some degree of openness of Mrs Clay; had appeared completely to see what Mrs Clay was about, and to hold her in contempt; and yet Mrs Clay found him as agreeable as any body.
PER

Mrs. John Knightley was a pretty, elegant little woman, of gentle, quiet manners, and a disposition remarkably amiable and affectionate; wrapt up in her family; a devoted wife, a doating mother, and so tenderly attached to her father and sister that, but for these higher ties, a warmer love might have seemed impossible.
EM

Anger

Angry people are not always wise.
PP

Annuities

"If you observe, people always live for ever when there is an annuity to be paid them; and she is very stout and healthy, and hardly forty. An annuity is a very serious busi-

ness; it comes over and over every year, and there is no getting rid of it. You are not aware of what you are doing. I have known a great deal of the trouble of annuities; for my mother was clogged with the payment of three to old superannuated servants by my father's will, and it is amazing how disagreeable she found it."
Fanny Dashwood, SS

Anxiety

Heavily passed the night. Sleep, or repose that deserved the Name of sleep, was out of the question. That room, in which her disturbed imagination had tormented her on her first arrival, was again the scene of agitated spirits and unquiet slumbers. Yet how different now the source of her inquietude from what it had been then—how mournfully superior in reality and substance! Her anxiety had foundation in fact, her fears in probability; and with a mind so occupied in the contemplation of actual and natural evil, the solitude of her situation, the darkness of her chamber, the antiquity of the building, were felt and considered without the smallest emotion; and though the wind was high, and often produced strange and sudden noises throughout the house, she heard it all as she lay awake, hour after hour, without curiosity or terror.
NA

She was safe; but peace and safety were unconnected here. Her mind had been never farther from peace. She could not feel that she had done wrong herself, but she was disquieted in every other way. Her heart and her judgment were equally against Edmund's decision: she could not acquit his unsteadiness, and his happiness under it made her wretched. She was full of jealousy and agitation.
MP

Appearance

He was a very good looking young man; height, air, address, all were unexceptionable, and his countenance had a great deal of the spirit and liveliness of his father's; he looked quick and sensible.
EM

His appearance is so much against him, and his manner so bad, that if she ever were disposed to favour him, she is not now.
EM

His manly beauty and more than common gracefulness were instantly the theme of general admiration, and the laugh which his gallantry raised against Marianne received particular spirit from his exterior attractions.
SS

They acknowledged considerable beauty; her features were pretty, and she had a sharp quick eye, and a smartness of air, which though it did not give actual elegance or grace, gave distinction to her person.
SS

"I shall very soon think him handsome, Elinor, if I do not now. When you tell me to love him as a brother, I shall no more see imperfection in his face, than I now do in his heart."
Marianne Dashwood, SS

Fanny Price was at this time just ten years old, and though there might not be much in her first appearance to captivate, there was, at least, nothing to disgust her relations. She was small of her age, with no glow of complexion, nor any other striking beauty; exceedingly timid and shy, and shrinking from notice; but her air, though awkward, was

not vulgar, her voice was sweet, and when she spoke her countenance was pretty.
MP

"There is hardly any personal defect," replied Anne, "which an agreeable manner might not gradually reconcile one to."
Anne Elliot, PER

Appearance and idleness

"In fact, as I have long been convinced, though every profession is necessary and honourable in its turn, it is only the lot of those who are not obliged to follow any, who can live in a regular way, in the country, choosing their own hours, following their own pursuits, and living on their own property, without the torment of trying for more; it is only their lot, I say, to hold the blessings of health and a good appearance to the utmost."
Mrs. Clay, PER

Appearances

"There is always a look of consciousness or bustle when people come in a way which they know to be beneath them."
Emma Woodhouse, EM

Art

They were viewing the country with the eyes of persons accustomed to drawing, and decided on its capability of being formed into pictures, with all the eagerness of real taste. Here Catherine was quite lost. She knew nothing of drawing—nothing of taste: and she listened to them with an attention which brought her little profit, for they talked in phrases which conveyed scarcely any idea to her. The little

which she could understand, however, appeared to contradict the very few notions she had entertained on the matter before. It seemed as if a good view were no longer to be taken from the top of an high hill, and that a clear blue sky was no longer a proof of a fine day. She was heartily ashamed of her ignorance.
NA

Artlessness

Artlessness will never do in Love matters; & that girl is born a simpleton who has it either by Nature or affectation. I am not yet certain that Reginald sees what she is about; nor is it of much consequence. She is now an object of indifference to him; she would be one of contempt were he to understand her Emotions.
LS

Attraction

"And till it appears that men are much more philosophic on the subject of beauty than they are generally supposed; till they do fall in love with well-informed minds instead of handsome faces, a girl, with such loveliness as Harriet, has a certainty of being admired and sought after, of having the power of chusing from among many, consequently a claim to be nice."
Emma Woodhouse, EM

Emma laughed, and replied, "My being charming, Harriet, is not quite enough to induce me to marry; I must find other people charming—one other person at least. And I am not only, not going to be married, at present, but have very little intention of ever marrying at all."
Emma Woodhouse, EM

"Miss Harriet Smith may not find offers of marriage flow in so fast, though she is a very pretty girl. Men of sense, whatever you may chuse to say, do not want silly wives."
George Knightley, EM

Captain Benwick and Louisa Musgrove! The high-spirited, joyous-talking Louisa Musgrove, and the dejected, thinking, feeling, reading, Captain Benwick, seemed each of them everything that would not suit the other. Their minds most dissimilar! Where could have been the attraction?
PER

Half the sum of attraction, on either side, might have been enough, for he had nothing to do, and she had hardly anybody to love; but the encounter of such lavish recommendations could not fail.
PER

She did not imagine that her father had at present an idea of the kind. Mrs. Clay had freckles, and a projecting tooth, and a clumsy wrist, which he was continually making severe remarks upon, in her absence; but she was young, and certainly altogether well-looking, and possessed, in an acute mind and assiduous pleasing manners, infinitely more dangerous attractions than any merely personal might have been.
PER

Aunts

His having been in love with the aunt gives . . . an additional interest . . . I like the idea—a very proper compliment to an aunt! I rather imagine indeed that nieces are seldom chosen but out of compliment to some aunt or another. I daresay Ben [Anna's husband] was in love with me once, and would never have thought of you, if he had not supposed me dead of a scarlet fever.
JAL

Now that you are become an Aunt, you are a person of some consequence and must excite great Interest in whatever you do. I have always maintained the importance of Aunts as much as possible, and am sure of your doing the same now.
JAL

Avoidance

Mrs. Gardiner went away in all the perplexity about Elizabeth and her Derbyshire friend that had attended her from that part of the world. His Name had never been voluntarily mentioned before them by her niece; and the kind of half-expectation which Mrs. Gardiner had formed, of their being followed by a letter from him, had ended in nothing.
PP

On the morning appointed for Admiral and Mrs. Croft's seeing Kellynch Hall, Anne found it most natural to take her almost daily walk to Lady Russell's, and keep out of the way till all was over; when she found it most Natural to be sorry that she had missed the opportunity of seeing them.
PER

Awkwardness

Elinor had just been congratulating herself, in the midst of her perplexity, that however difficult it might be to express herself properly by letter, it was at least preferable to giving the information by word of mouth . . .
SS

He spoke to her, and then turned away. The character of his manner was embarrassment. She could not have called it ei-

ther cold or friendly, or anything so certainly as embarrassed.
PER

Babies

I give you joy of our new nephew, and hope if he ever comes to be hanged, it will not be till we are too old to care about it.
JAL

Bad Habits

She saw that there had been bad habits; that Sunday travelling had been a common thing.
PER

Beauty

"Such an eye!—the true hazel eye—and so brilliant! regular features, open countenance, with a complexion! oh! what a bloom of full health, and such a pretty height and size; such a firm and upright figure! There is health, not merely in her bloom, but in her air, her head, her glance.
Mrs. Weston, EM

Beauty and plainness

To look *almost* pretty, is an acquisition of higher delight to a girl who has been looking plain the first fifteen years of her life, than a beauty from her cradle can ever receive.
NA

Beauty of complexion

"Did you ever see such a skin?—such smoothness! such delicacy!—and yet without being actually fair.—One cannot call her fair. It is a most uncommon complexion, with her dark eye-lashes and hair—a most distinguishing complexion! Just colour enough for beauty."
Frank Churchill, EM

Beauty of one's beloved

"She is a complete angel. Look at her. Is not she an angel in every gesture? Observe the turn of her throat. Observe her eyes."
Frank Churchill, EM

Beauty, once youth has passed

[I] am very well satisfied with his notice of me—"A pleasing-looking young woman"—that must do; one cannot pretend to anything better now; thankful to have it continued a few years longer!
JAL

Inequities of beauty

Lady Bertram listened without much interest to this sort of invective. She could not enter into the wrongs of an economist, but she felt all the injuries of beauty in Mrs. Grant's being so well settled in life without being handsome, and expressed her astonishment on that point almost as often, though not so diffusely, as Mrs. Norris discussed the other.
MP

Real beauty

Marianne was still handsomer. Her form, though not so correct as her sister's, in having the advantage of height, was more striking; and her face was so lovely, that when in the common cant of praise, she was called a beautiful girl, truth was less violently outraged than usually happens.
SS
Frank Churchill, EM

Uncle's opinion

"Your uncle thinks you very pretty, dear Fanny—and that is the long and the short of the matter. Anybody but myself would have made something more of it, and anybody but you would resent that you had not been thought very pretty before; but the truth is, that your uncle never did admire you till now—and now he does. Your complexion is so improved!—and you have gained so much countenance!—and your figure—Fanny, do not turn away about it—it is but an uncle. If you cannot bear an uncle's admiration, what is to become of you? You must really begin to harden yourself to the idea of being worth looking at. You must try not to mind growing up into a pretty woman."
Edmund Bertram, MP

Becoming a Woman

Instead of falling a sacrifice to an irresistible passion, as once she had fondly flattered herself with expecting,—instead of remaining even for ever with her mother, and finding her only pleasures in retirement and study, as afterwards in her more calm and sober judgment she had determined on,—she found herself at nineteen, submitting to new attachments, entering on new duties, placed in a new home, a wife, the mistress of a family, and the patroness of a village.
SS

Betrayal

With what indignation such a letter as this must be read by Miss Dashwood, may be imagined. Though aware, before she began it, that it must bring a confession of his inconstancy, and confirm their separation for ever, she was not aware that such language could be suffered to announce it; nor could she have supposed Willoughby capable of departing so far from the appearance of every honourable and delicate feeling—so far from the common decorum of a gentleman, as to send a letter so impudently cruel: a letter which, instead of bringing with his desire of a release any professions of regret, acknowledged no breach of faith, denied all peculiar affection whatever—a letter of which every line was an insult, and which proclaimed its writer to be deep in hardened villainy.
SS

"It is too much! Oh, Willoughby, Willoughby, could this be yours! Cruel, cruel—nothing can acquit you. Elinor, nothing can. Whatever he might have heard against me—ought he not to have suspended his belief? ought he not to have told me of it, to have given me the power of clearing myself? 'The lock of hair, repeating it from the letter, which you so obligingly bestowed on me'—That is unpardonable. Willoughby, where was your heart when you wrote those words? Oh, barbarously insolent!"
Marianne Dashwood, SS

Black Sheep

The Musgroves had had the ill fortune of a very troublesome, hopeless son; and the good fortune to lose him before he reached his twentieth year; that he had been sent to sea because he was stupid and unmanageable on shore; that he

had been very little cared for at any time by his family, though quite as much as he deserved; seldom heard of, and scarcely at all regretted.
PER

Bliss

This indulgence, though not more than Catherine had hoped for, completed her conviction of being favoured beyond every other human creature, in friends and fortune, circumstance and chance. Everything seemed to cooperate for her advantage. By the kindness of her first friends, the Allens, she had been introduced into scenes where pleasures of every kind had met her. Her feelings, her preferences, had each known the happiness of a return.
NA

Boredom

"That she should be tired now, however, gives me no surprise; for there is nothing in the course of one's duties so fatiguing as what we have been doing this morning: seeing a great house, dawdling from one room to another, straining one's eyes and one's attention, hearing what one does not understand, admiring what one does not care for. It is generally allowed to be the greatest bore in the world, and Miss Price has found it so, though she did not know it."
Mary Crawford, MP

Bores

Having been a valetudinarian all his life, without activity of mind or body, he was a much older man in ways than in

years; and though everywhere beloved for the friendliness of his heart and his amiable temper, his talents could not have recommended him at any time.
EM

The quiet prosings of three such women made her feel that every evening so spent was indeed one of the long evenings she had fearfully anticipated.
EM

"Brandon is just the kind of man," said Willoughby one day, when they were talking of him together, "whom every body speaks well of, and nobody cares about; whom all are delighted to see, and nobody remembers to talk to."
John Willoughby, SS

Little as Catherine was in the habit of judging for herself, and unfixed as were her general notions of what men ought to be, she could not entirely repress a doubt, while she bore with the effusions of his endless conceit, of his being altogether completely agreeable. It was a bold surmise, for he was Isabella's brother; and she had been assured by James that his manners would recommend him to all her sex; but in spite of this, the extreme weariness of his company, which crept over her before they had been out an hour, and which continued unceasingly to increase till they stopped in Pulteney Street again, induced her, in some small degree, to resist such high authority, and to distrust his powers of giving universal pleasure.
NA

No poverty of any kind, except of conversation, appeared— but there, the deficiency was considerable. John Dashwood had not much to say for himself that was worth hearing, and his wife had still less. But there was no peculiar disgrace in this; for it was very much the case with the chief of their visitors, who almost all laboured under one or other of

these disqualifications for being agreeable—Want of sense, either Natural or improved—want of elegance—want of spirits—or want of temper.
SS

Breakup

"You must not talk so, Marianne. Have you no comforts? no friends? Is your loss such as leaves no opening for consolation? Much as you suffer now, think of what you would have suffered if the discovery of his character had been delayed to a later period—if your engagement had been carried on for months and months, as it might have been, before he chose to put an end to it. Every additional day of unhappy confidence, on your side, would have made the blow more dreadful."
Elinor Dashwood, SS

Breeding

Every qualification is raised at times, by the circumstances of the moment, to more than its real value; and she was sometimes worried down by officious condolence to rate good-breeding as more indispensable to comfort than good-nature.
SS

Brevity

After long thought and much perplexity, to be very brief was all that she could determine on with any confidence of safety.
NA

Brides

"No, my dear, I never encouraged any body to marry, but I would always wish to pay every proper attention to a lady—and a bride, especially, is never to be neglected. More is avowedly due to her. A bride, you know, my dear, is always the first in company, let the others be who they may."
Mr. Woodhouse, EM

Brokenheartedness

They saw nothing of Marianne till dinner time, when she entered the room and took her place at the table without saying a word. Her eyes were red and swollen; and it seemed as if her tears were even then restrained with difficulty. She avoided the looks of them all, could neither eat nor speak, and after some time, on her mother's silently pressing her hand with tender compassion, her small degree of fortitude was quite overcome, she burst into tears and left the room.
SS

Brothers

The younger brother must help to pay for the pleasures of the elder.
MP

Cads

I have seen Sir James; he came to Town for a few days last week, & called several times in Edward Street. I talked to him about you & your Daughter, & he is so far from having forgotten you, that I am sure he would marry either of you

with pleasure. I gave him hopes of Frederica's relenting, & told him a great deal of her improvements. I scolded him for making Love to Maria Manwaring; he protested that he had been only in joke, & we both laughed heartily at her disappointment; and, in short, were very agreable. He is as silly as ever.
LS

Willoughby, he, whom only half an hour ago she had abhorred as the most worthless of men, Willoughby, in spite of all his faults, excited a degree of commiseration for the sufferings produced by them, which made her think of him as now separated for ever from her family, with a tenderness, a regret, rather in proportion, as she soon acknowledged within herself—to his wishes than to his merits.
SS

Caprice

"She will never submit to any thing requiring industry and patience, and a subjection of the fancy to the understanding."
George Knightley, EM

Vanity, extravagance, love of change, restlessness of temper, which must be doing something, good or bad; heedlessness as to the pleasure of his father and Mrs. Weston, indifferent as to how his conduct might appear in general; he became liable to all these charges.
EM

Chance

But while the imaginations of other people will carry them away to form wrong judgments of our conduct, and to de-

cide on it by slight appearances, one's happiness must in some measure be always at the mercy of chance.
SS

Character

"I cannot rate her beauty as you do," said he; "but she is a pretty little creature, and I am inclined to think very well of her disposition. Her character depends upon those she is with; but in good hands she will turn out a valuable woman."
George Knightley, EM

"He has too much real feeling to address any woman on the haphazard of selfish passion. And as to conceit, he is the farthest from it of any man I know."
George Knightley, EM

Mrs. Bennet was restored to her usual querulous serenity.
PP

She was a benevolent, charitable, good woman, and capable of strong attachments, most correct in her conduct, strict in her notions of decorum, and with manners that were held a standard of good-breeding.
PER

"It does not follow that a deep, intricate character is more or less estimable than such a one as yours . . ."
    "I did not know before," continued Bingley immediately, "that you were a studier of character. It must be an amusing study."
    "Yes; but intricate characters are the *most* amusing. They have at least that advantage."
Elizabeth Bennet, Charles Bingley, PP

Lady Elliot had been an excellent woman, sensible and amiable; whose judgement and conduct, if they might be pardoned the youthful infatuation which made her Lady Elliot, had never required indulgence afterwards.—She had humoured, or softened, or concealed his failings, and promoted his real respectability for seventeen years; and though not the very happiest being in the world herself, had found enough in her duties, her friends, and her children, to attach her to life, and make it no matter of indifference to her when she was called on to quit them.
PER

Charity

Elizabeth soon perceived that though this great lady . . . was a most active magistrate in her own parish . . . whenever any of the cottagers were disposed to be quarrelsome, discontented or too poor, she sallied forth into the village to settle their differences, silence their complaints, and scold them into harmony and plenty.
PP

Charm

She felt that his influence over her mind was heightened by circumstances which ought not in reason to have weight; by that person of uncommon attraction, that open, affectionate, and lively manner which it was no merit to possess.
SS

"There is no charm equal to tenderness of heart."
Emma Woodhouse, EM

Children

As to the management of their children, his theory was much better than his wife's, and his practice not so bad. "I could manage them very well, if it were not for Mary's interference," was what Anne often heard him say, and had a good deal of faith in; but when listening in turn to Mary's reproach of "Charles spoils the children so that I cannot get them into any order," she never had the smallest temptation to say, "Very true."
PER

In vain were the well-meant condescensions of Sir Thomas, and all the officious prognostications of Mrs. Norris that she would be a good girl; in vain did Lady Bertram smile and make her sit on the sofa with herself and pug, and vain was even the sight of a gooseberry tart towards giving her comfort; she could scarcely swallow two mouthfuls before tears interrupted her, and sleep seeming to be her likeliest friend, she was taken to finish her sorrows in bed.
MP

On every formal visit a child ought to be of the party, by way of provision for discourse.
SS

Give my love to little Cassandra! I hope she found my bed comfortable last night and has not filled it with fleas.
JAL

Chills

The wind roared down the chimney, the rain beat in torrents against the windows, and everything seemed to speak the awfulness of her situation. . . . The storm still raged, and various were the noises, more terrific even than the wind,

which struck at intervals on her startled ear. The very curtains of her bed seemed at one moment in motion, and at another the lock of her door was agitated, as if by the attempt of somebody to enter. Hollow murmurs seemed to creep along the gallery, and more than once her blood was chilled by the sound of distant moans.
NA

Church

"For what is to be done in the church? Men love to distinguish themselves, and in either of the other lines distinction may be gained, but not in the church."
Mary Crawford, MP

They entered. Fanny's imagination had prepared her for something grander than a mere spacious, oblong room, fitted up for the purpose of devotion: with nothing more striking or more solemn than the profusion of mahogany, and the crimson velvet cushions appearing over the ledge of the family gallery above. "I am disappointed," said she, in a low voice, to Edmund. "This is not my idea of a chapel. There is nothing awful here, nothing melancholy, nothing grand. Here are no aisles, no arches, no inscriptions, no banners. No banners, cousin, to be 'blown by the night wind of heaven.' No signs that a 'Scottish monarch sleeps below.'"
Fanny Price, MP

Church attendance

Everybody likes to go their own way—to chuse their own time and manner of devotion. The obligation of attendance, the formality, the restraint, the length of time—altogether it is a formidable thing, and what nobody likes; if the good people who used to kneel and gape in that gallery could

have foreseen that the time would ever come when men and women might lie another ten minutes in bed, when they woke with a headache, without danger of reprobation, because chapel was missed, they would have jumped with joy and envy.
MP

Clergy

"A clergyman is nothing."

"The *nothing* of conversation has its gradations, I hope, as well as the *never*. A clergyman cannot be high in state or fashion. He must not head mobs, or set the ton in dress. But I cannot call that situation nothing which has the charge of all that is of the first importance to mankind, individually or collectively considered, temporally and eternally, which has the guardianship of religion and morals, and consequently of the manners which result from their influence. No one here can call the *office* nothing. If the man who holds it is so, it is by the neglect of his duty, by foregoing its just importance, and stepping out of his place to appear what he ought not to appear."
Mary Crawford, Edmund Bertram, MP

He laughed most immoderately. The idea of Edward's being a clergyman, and living in a small parsonage-house, diverted him beyond measure;—and when to that was added the fanciful imagery of Edward reading prayers in a white surplice, and publishing the banns of marriage between John Smith and Mary Brown, he could conceive nothing more ridiculous.
SS

"A fine preacher is followed and admired; but it is not in fine preaching only that a good clergyman will be useful in

his parish and his neighbourhood, where the parish and neighbourhood are of a size capable of knowing his private character, and observing his general conduct."
Edmund Bertram, MP

"I must beg some advantage to the clergyman from your own argument. As he cannot be influenced by those feelings which you rank highly as temptation and reward to the soldier and sailor in their choice of a profession, as heroism, and noise, and fashion, are all against him, he ought to be less liable to the suspicion of wanting sincerity or good intentions in the choice of his."
Edmund Bertram, MP

"Oh! no doubt he is very sincere in preferring an income ready made, to the trouble of working for one; and has the best intentions of doing nothing all the rest of his days but eat, drink, and grow fat. . . . A clergyman has nothing to do but be slovenly and selfish—read the newspaper, watch the weather, and quarrel with his wife. His curate does all the work, and the business of his own life is to dine."
Mary Crawford, MP

Common Sense

"But as it is—you must not let your fancy run away with you. You have sense, and we all expect you to use it."
Mrs. Gardiner, PP

Commonness

Nothing was wanting on Mrs. Palmer's side that constant and friendly good humour could do, to make them feel themselves welcome. The openness and heartiness of her manner more than atoned for that want of recollection and

elegance which made her often deficient in the forms of politeness; her kindness, recommended by so pretty a face, was engaging; her folly, though evident was not disgusting, because it was not conceited; and Elinor could have forgiven every thing but her laugh.
SS

Compassion

[He] entered into conversation with her, in a low voice, about her son, doing it with so much sympathy and Natural grace, as shewed the kindest consideration for all that was real and unabsurd in the parent's feelings.
PER

He could not forgive her, but he could not be unfeeling. Though condemning her for the past, and considering it with high and unjust resentment, though perfectly careless of her, and though becoming attached to another, still he could not see her suffer, without the desire of giving her relief. It was a remainder of former sentiment; it was an impulse of pure, though unacknowledged friendship; it was a proof of his own warm and amiable heart.
PER

Complaining

"Those who do not complain are never pitied."
Mrs. Bennet, PP

Compliments

It is something for a woman to be assured, in her eight-and-twentieth year, that she has not lost one charm of earlier

youth; but the value of such homage was inexpressibly increased to Anne, by comparing it with former words, and feeling it to be the result, not the cause of a revival of his warm attachment.
PER

Constancy

"It would not be the Nature of any woman who truly loved."
Captain Harville smiled, as much as to say, "Do you claim that for your sex?" and she answered the question, smiling also, "Yes. We certainly do not forget you as soon as you forget us. It is, perhaps, our fate rather than our merit. We cannot help ourselves. We live at home, quiet, confined, and our feelings prey upon us. You are forced on exertion. You have always a profession, pursuits, business of some sort or other, to take you back into the world immediately, and continual occupation and change soon weaken impressions."
Anne Elliot, Captain Harville, PER

Conversation

"*Never* is a black word. But yes, in the *never* of conversation, which means *not very often*, I do think it."
Mary Crawford, MP

You distress me cruelly by your request about books. I cannot think of any to bring with me, nor have I any idea of our wanting them. I come to you to be talked to, not to read or hear reading; I can do *that* at home; and indeed I am now laying in a stock of intelligence to pour out on you as *my* share of the conversation.
—JAL

Country Versus Town

"The country," said Darcy, "can in general supply but few subjects for such a study. In a country neighbourhood you move in a very confined and unvarying society."

"But people themselves alter so much, that there is something new to be observed in them for ever."

"Yes, indeed," cried Mrs. Bennet, offended by his manner of mentioning a country neighbourhood. "I assure you there is quite as much of *that* going on in the country as in town." Every body was surprised; and Darcy, after looking at her for a moment, turned silently away. Mrs. Bennet, who fancied she had gained a complete victory over him, continued her triumph.

"I cannot see that London has any great advantage over the country for my part, except the shops and public places. The country is a vast deal pleasanter, is not it, Mr. Bingley?"

"When I am in the country," he replied, "I never wish to leave it; and when I am in town it is pretty much the same. They have each their advantages, and I can be equally happy in either."

Fitzwilliam Darcy, Elizabeth Bennet, Mrs. Bennet,
Charles Bingley, PP

The sun's rays falling strongly into the parlour, instead of cheering, made her still more melancholy, for sunshine appeared to her a totally different thing in a town and in the country. Here, its power was only a glare: a stifling, sickly glare, serving but to bring forward stains and dirt that might otherwise have slept. There was neither health nor gaiety in sunshine in a town.

MP

Courage

"My courage always rises at every attempt to intimidate me."
Elizabeth Bennet, PP

Courtship

"Cautious, very cautious," thought Emma; "he advances inch by inch, and will hazard nothing till he believes himself secure."
Emma Woodhouse, EM

"There is so much of gratitude or vanity in almost every attachment, that it is not safe to leave any to itself. We can all *begin* freely—a slight preference is Natural enough; but there are very few of us who have heart enough to be really in love without encouragement. In nine cases out of ten, a woman had better shew *more* affection than she feels."
Charlotte Lucas, PP

Cousins

Sir John wanted the whole family to walk to the Park directly and look at his guests. Benevolent, philanthropic man! It was painful to him even to keep a third cousin to himself.
SS

Coyness

"I refused him as long as I possibly could, but he would take no denial. You have no idea how he pressed me. I

begged him to excuse me, and get some other partner—but no, not he; after aspiring to my hand, there was nobody else in the room he could bear to think of; and it was not that he wanted merely to dance, he wanted to be with me. Oh! Such nonsense! I told him he had taken a very unlikely way to prevail upon me; for, of all things in the world, I hated fine speeches and compliments; and so—and so then I found there would be no peace if I did not stand up.... I am so glad it is over! My spirits are quite jaded with listening to his nonsense."
Isabella Thorpe, NA

With Tuesday came the agreeable prospect of seeing him again, and for a longer time than hitherto; of judging of his general manners, and by inference, of the meaning of his manners towards herself; of guessing how soon it might be necessary for her to throw coldness into her air; and of fancying what the observations of all those might be, who were now seeing them together for the first time.
EM

Edward assured them himself of his being in town, within a very short time, by twice calling in Berkeley Street. Twice was his card found on the table, when they returned from their morning's engagements. Elinor was pleased that he had called; and still more pleased that she had missed him.
SS

Critics

I ... do not think the worse of him for having a brain so very different from mine.... And he deserves better treatment than to be obliged to read any more of my works.
JAL

Ladies who read those enormous great stupid thick quarto volumes which one always sees in the breakfast parlour there must be acquainted with everything in the world. I detest a quarto. Capt. Pasley's book is too good for their society. They will not understand a man who condenses his thoughts into an octavo.
JAL

Cruelty

With silent indignation, Fanny repeated to herself, "Never happier!—never happier than when doing what you must know was not justifiable!—never happier than when behaving so dishonourably and unfeelingly! Oh! what a corrupted mind!"
MP

Dancing

"By the bye, Charles, are you really serious in meditating a dance at Netherfield?—I would advise you, before you determine on it, to consult the wishes of the present party; I am much mistaken if there are not some among us to whom a ball would be rather a punishment than a pleasure."
Caroline Bingley, PP

"There is nothing like dancing after all. I consider it as one of the first refinements of polished society."
    "Certainly, sir; and it has the advantage also of being in vogue amongst the less polished societies of the world. Every savage can dance."
Sir William Lucas, Fitzwilliam Darcy, PP

Dancing and flirting

"Do not you feel a great inclination, Miss Bennet, to seize such an opportunity of dancing a reel?"

She smiled, but made no answer. He repeated the question, with some surprise at her silence.

"Oh!" said she, "I heard you before; but I could not immediately determine what to say in reply. You wanted me, I know, to say 'Yes,' that you might have the pleasure of despising my taste; but I always delight in overthrowing those kind of schemes, and cheating a person of their premeditated contempt. I have therefore made up my mind to tell you that I do not want to dance a reel at all—and now despise me if you dare."

Fitzwilliam Darcy, Elizabeth Bennet, PP

Dancing and health

"Open the windows!—but surely, Mr. Churchill, nobody would think of opening the windows at Randalls. Nobody could be so imprudent! I never heard of such a thing. Dancing with open windows!"

Mr. Woodhouse, EM

Dancing and lateness

She could not help being vexed at the non-appearance of Mr. Thorpe, for she not only longed to be dancing, but was likewise aware that, as the real dignity of her situation could not be known, she was sharing with the scores of other young ladies still sitting down all the discredit of wanting a partner.

NA

Dancing and love

To be fond of dancing was a certain step towards falling in love.
PP

Dancing and marriage

"We have entered into a contract of mutual agreeableness for the space of an evening, and all our agreeableness belongs solely to each other for that time. Nobody can fasten themselves on the notice of one, without injuring the rights of the other. I consider a country-dance as an emblem of marriage. Fidelity and complaisance are the principal duties of both; and those men who do not choose to dance or marry themselves, have no business with the partners or wives of their neighbors."

"But they are such very different things!—"

"—That you think they cannot be compared together."

"To be sure not. People that marry can never part, but must go and keep house together. People that dance, only stand opposite each other in a long room for half an hour."

"And such is your definition of matrimony and dancing. Taken in that light certainly, their resemblance is not striking; but I think I could place them in such a view.—You will allow, that in both, man has the advantage of choice, woman only the power of refusal; that in both, it is an engagement between man and woman, formed for the advantage of each; and that when once entered into, they belong exclusively to each other till the moment of its dissolution; that it is their duty, each to endeavor to give the other no cause for wishing that he or she had bestowed themselves elsewhere, and their best interest to keep their own imaginations from wandering towards the perfections of their neighbours, or fancying that they should have been better off with anyone else."
Henry Tilney, Catherine Morland, NA

Doing without dancing

It may be possible to do without dancing entirely. Instances have been known of young people passing many, many months successively, without being at any ball of any description, and no material injury accrue either to body or mind;—but when a beginning is made—when the felicities of rapid motion have once been, though slightly, felt—it must be a very heavy set that does not ask for more.
EM

Watching others dance

"Pleasure in seeing dancing!—not I, indeed—I never look at it—I do not know who does.—Fine dancing, I believe, like virtue, must be its own reward. Those who are standing by are usually thinking of something very different."
George Knightley, EM

Dashed Hopes

It was a wretched business indeed!—Such an overthrow of every thing she had been wishing for!—Such a development of every thing most unwelcome!—
EM

Debt

While Lady Elliot lived, there had been method, moderation, and economy, which had just kept him within his income; but with her had died all such right-mindedness, and from that period he had been constantly exceeding it. It had not been possible for him to spend less; he had done noth-

ing but what Sir Walter Elliot was imperiously called on to do; but blameless as he was, he was not only growing dreadfully in debt, but was hearing of it so often, that it became vain to attempt concealing it longer, even partially, from his daughter.
PER

Décor

The room was most dear to her, and she would not have changed its furniture for the handsomest in the house, though what had been originally plain had suffered all the ill-usage of children; and its greatest elegancies and ornaments were a faded footstool of Julia's work, too ill done for the drawing-room, three transparencies, made in a rage for transparencies, for the three lower panes of one window, where Tintern Abbey held its station between a cave in Italy and a moonlight lake in Cumberland, a collection of family profiles, thought unworthy of being anywhere else, over the mantelpiece, and by their side, and pinned against the wall, a small sketch of a ship sent four years ago from the Mediterranean by William, with H.M.S. Antwerp at the bottom, in letters as tall as the mainmast.
MP

They had the pleasure of assuring her that Bath more than answered their expectations in every respect. Their house was undoubtedly the best in Camden Place; their drawing-rooms had many decided advantages over all the others which they had either seen or heard of, and the superiority was not less in the style of the fitting-up, or the taste of the furniture.
PER

Depression

At the bottom of Kingsdown Hill we met a gentleman in a buggy, who, on minute examination, turned out to be Dr. Hall—and Dr. Hall in such very deep mourning that either his mother, his wife, or himself must be dead.
JAL

Despair

The state of her spirits had probably had its share in her indisposition; for she had been feeling neglected, and been struggling against discontent and envy for some days past. As she leant on the sofa, to which she had retreated that she might not be seen, the pain of her mind had been much beyond that in her head; and the sudden change which Edmund's kindness had then occasioned, made her hardly know how to support herself.
MP

He had told her the most extraordinary, the most inconceivable, the most unwelcome news; and she could think of nothing else. To be acting! After all his objections—objections so just and so public! After all that she had heard him say, and seen him look, and known him to be feeling. Could it be possible? Edmund so inconsistent! Was he not deceiving himself? Was he not wrong? Alas! it was all Miss Crawford's doing. She had seen her influence in every speech, and was miserable. The doubts and alarms as to her own conduct, which had previously distressed her, and which had all slept while she listened to him, were become of little consequence now. This deeper anxiety swallowed them up. Things should take their course; she cared not how it ended. Her cousins might attack, but could hardly tease

her. She was beyond their reach; and if at last obliged to
yield—no matter—it was all misery *now*.
MP

Desserts

You know how interesting the purchase of a sponge-cake is
to me.
JAL

Devotion

Marianne could never love by halves; and her whole heart
became, in time, as much devoted to her husband, as it had
once been to Willoughby.
SS

Dinner Parties

Dinner passed away; the dessert succeeded, the children
came in, and were talked to and admired amid the usual
rate of conversation; a few clever things said, a few downright silly, but by much the larger proportion neither the
one nor the other—nothing worse than everyday remarks,
dull repetitions, old news, and heavy jokes.
EM

To be sitting long after dinner, was a confinement that he
could not endure. Neither wine nor conversation was any
thing to him.
EM

At length, however, Mrs. Bennet had no more to say; and Lady Lucas, who had been long yawning at the repetition of delights which she saw no likelihood of sharing, was left to the comforts of cold ham and chicken. Elizabeth now began to revive. But not long was the interval of tranquillity; for when supper was over, singing was talked of, and she had the mortification of seeing Mary, after very little entreaty, preparing to oblige the company.
PP

Disappointment

"I am very sorry to be right in this instance. I would much rather have been merry than wise."
Emma Woodhouse, EM

Poor Marianne, languid and low from the Nature of her malady, and feeling herself universally ill, could no longer hope that tomorrow would find her recovered; and the idea of what tomorrow would have produced, but for this unlucky illness, made every ailment severe; for on that day they were to have begun their journey home; and, attended the whole way by a servant of Mrs. Jennings, were to have taken their mother by surprise on the following forenoon.
SS

Disdain

There was not a baronet from A to Z whom her feelings could have so willingly acknowledged as an equal. Yet so miserably had he conducted himself, that though she was at this present time wearing black ribbons for his wife, she could not admit him to be worth thinking of again.
PER

Disillusionment

He had not forgiven Anne Elliot. She had used him ill, deserted and disappointed him; and worse, she had shewn a feebleness of character in doing so, which his own decided, confident temper could not endure. She had given him up to oblige others. It had been the effect of over-persuasion. It had been weakness and timidity. He had been most warmly attached to her, and had never seen a woman since whom he thought her equal; but, except from some Natural sensation of curiosity, he had no desire of meeting her again. Her power with him was gone for ever.
PER

Disinheritance

"Yet why, upon her late behavior, is she supposed to feel at all?—She has done with her son, she cast him off for ever, and has made all those over whom she had any influence, cast him off likewise. Surely, after doing so, she cannot be imagined liable to any impression of sorrow or of joy on his account—she cannot be interested in any thing that befalls him.—She would not be so weak as to throw away the comfort of a child, and yet retain the anxiety of a parent!"
Elinor Dashwood, SS

Dislike

It was a dislike which not all his fortune and consequence might do away.
PP

The confidential discourse of the two ladies was therefore at an end, to which both of them submitted without any

reluctance, for nothing had been said on either side to make them dislike each other less than they had done before.
SS

But while she smiled at a graciousness so misapplied, she could not reflect on the mean-spirited folly from which it sprung, nor observe the studied attentions with which the Miss Steeles courted its continuance, without thoroughly despising them all four.
SS

"I meant to be uncommonly clever in taking so decided a dislike to him, without any reason. It is such a spur to one's genius, such an opening for wit to have a dislike of that kind. One may be continually abusive without saying any thing just; but one cannot be always laughing at a man without now and then stumbling on something witty."
Elizabeth Bennet, PP

Fanny Austen's match is quite news, and I am sorry she has behaved so ill. There is some comfort to us in her misconduct, that we have not a congratulatory letter to write.
JAL

I do not like the Miss Blackstones; indeed, I was always determined not to like them, so there is the less merit in it.
JAL

She was not a woman of many words; for, unlike people in general, she proportioned them to the number of her ideas; and of the few syllables that did escape her, not one fell to the share of Miss Dashwood, whom she eyed with the spirited determination of disliking her at all events.
SS

She wished him very well; but he gave her pain, and his welfare twenty miles off would administer most satisfaction.
EM

Though nothing could be more polite than Lady Middleton's behaviour to Elinor and Marianne, she did not really like them at all. Because they neither flattered herself nor her children, she could not believe them good-natured; and because they were fond of reading, she fancied them satirical: perhaps without exactly knowing what it was to be satirical; but THAT did not signify. It was censure in common use, and easily given.
SS

Disposition

He considered his disposition as of the sort which must suffer heavily, uniting very strong feelings with quiet, serious, and retiring manners, and a decided taste for reading, and sedentary pursuits.
PER

Disrespect

"I am not going to urge her," replied Mrs. Norris sharply; "but I shall think her a very obstinate, ungrateful girl, if she does not do what her aunt and cousins wish her—very ungrateful, indeed, considering who and what she is."
Mrs. Norris, MP

Distractions

The nonsense I have been writing in this and in my last letter seems out of place at such a time, but I will not mind it; it will do you no harm, and nobody else will be attacked by it.
JAL

Distress

"It might be distressing, for the moment," said she; "but you seem to have behaved extremely well; and it is over— and may never—can never, as a first meeting, occur again, and therefore you need not think about it."
—Emma Woodhouse, EM

Dreams

"What an air of probability sometimes runs through a dream! And at others, what a heap of absurdities it is!"
Mr. Weston, EM

Dress

Mrs. Powlett was at once expensively nakedly dress'd; we have had the satisfaction of estimating her Lace & her Muslin; & she said too little to afford us much other amusement.
JAL

What gown and what head-dress she should wear on the occasion became her chief concern. She cannot be justified in it. Dress is at all times a frivolous distinction, and excessive solicitude about it often destroys its own aim. Catherine knew all this very well; her great aunt had read her a lecture on the subject only the Christmas before; and yet she lay awake ten minutes on Wednesday night debating between her spotted and her tamboured muslin, and nothing but the shortness of the time prevented her buying a new one for the evening.

NA

Drinking

She believed he had been drinking too much of Mr. Weston's good wine, and felt sure that he would want to be talking nonsense.

EM

Drunkenness

Mrs. B. and two young women were of the same party, except when Mrs. B. thought herself obliged to leave them to run round the room after her drunken husband. His avoidance, and her pursuit, with the probable intoxication of both, was an amusing scene.

JAL

Duels

One most material comfort, however, they have; the assurance of its being really an accidental wound, which is not only positively declared by Earle himself, but is likewise testified by the particular direction of the bullet. Such a wound could not have been received in a duel.

JAL

Duty

"I am afraid," replied Elinor, "that the pleasantness of an employment does not always evince its propriety."
Elinor Dashwood, SS

"There is one thing, Emma, which a man can always do, if he chuses, and that is, his duty; not by manoeuvring and finessing, but by vigour and resolution."
George Knightley, EM

"What is right to be done cannot be done too soon."
Mr. Weston, EM

Dying Love

Elinor saw, with great uneasiness the low spirits of her friend. His visit afforded her but a very partial satisfaction, while his own enjoyment in it appeared so imperfect. It was evident that he was unhappy; she wished it were equally evident that he still distinguished her by the same affection which once she had felt no doubt of inspiring; but hitherto the continuance of his preference seemed very uncertain; and the reservedness of his manner towards her contradicted one moment what a more animated look had intimated the preceding one.
SS

Education

[It was] a real, honest, old-fashioned Boarding-school, where a reasonable quantity of accomplishments were sold at a reasonable price, and where girls might be sent to be out of

the way, and scramble themselves into a little education, without any danger of coming back prodigies.
EM

"Give a girl an education, and introduce her properly into the world, and ten to one but she has the means of settling well, without farther expense to anybody."
Mrs. Norris, MP

. . . it is not very wonderful that, with all their promising talents and early information, they should be entirely deficient in the less common acquirements of self-knowledge, generosity and humility. In everything but disposition they were admirably taught.
MP

"You think me foolish to call instruction a torment, but if you have been as much used as myself to hear poor little children first learning their letters and then learning to spell, if you had ever seen how stupid they can be for a whole morning together, and how tired my poor mother is at the end of it, as I am in the habit of seeing almost every day of my life at home, you would allow that to torment and to instruct might sometimes be used as synonymous words."
Catherine Morland, NA

She looks very well, and her hair is done up with an elegance to do credit to any education. Her manners are as unaffected and pleasing as ever. . . . I was shewn upstairs into a drawing-room, where she came to me, and the appearance of the room, so totally unschool-like, amused me very much; it was full of modern elegancies, and if it had not been for some naked cupids over the mantlepiece, which must be a fine study for girls, one should never have smelt instruction.
JAL

Education and character

"There is in every disposition a tendency to some particular evil, a Natural defect, which not even the best education can overcome."
Fitzwilliam Darcy, PP

Governesses

"We never had any governess."

"No governess! How was that possible? Five daughters brought up at home without a governess!—I never heard of such a thing. Your mother must have been quite a slave to your education."

Elizabeth could hardly help smiling, as she assured her that had not been the case.

"Then, who taught you? who attended to you? Without a governess you must have been neglected."

"Compared with some families, I believe we were; but such of us as wished to learn, never wanted the means. We were always encouraged to read, and had all the masters that were necessary. Those who chose to be idle, certainly might."

"Aye, no doubt; but that is what a governess will prevent, and if I had known your mother, I should have advised her most strenuously to engage one. I always say that nothing is to be done in education without steady and regular instruction, and nobody but a governess can give it."
Elizabeth Bennet, Lady Catherine de Bourgh, PP

Elegance

"I have no pretensions whatever to that kind of elegance which consists in tormenting a respectable man."
Elizabeth Bennet, PP

What dreadful hot weather we have! It keeps me in a continual state of inelegance.
JAL

But it had passed as his way, as a mere error of judgment, of knowledge, of taste, as one proof among others that he had not always lived in the best society, that with all the gentleness of his address, true elegance was sometimes wanting.
EM

Elopement

Alas! why do you thus so cruelly connive at the projected Misery of her and of yourself by delaying to communicate that scheme which had doubtless long possessed your imagination? A secret Union will at once secure the felicity of both.
LF

Embarrassment

She had not seen him before since his engagement became public, and therefore not since his knowing her to be acquainted with it; which, with the consciousness of what she had been thinking of, and what she had to tell him, made her feel particularly uncomfortable for some minutes. He too was much distressed; and they sat down together in a most promising state of embarrassment.
SS

Emotion

He was more obviously struck and confused by the sight of her than she had ever observed before; he looked quite red.

For the first time, since their renewed acquaintance, she felt that she was betraying the least sensibility of the two. She had the advantage of him in the preparation of the last few moments. All the overpowering, blinding, bewildering, first effects of strong surprise were over with her. Still, however, she had enough to feel! It was agitation, pain, pleasure, a something between delight and misery.

PER

The circumstances of the morning had led Catherine's feelings through the varieties of suspense, security, and disappointment; but they were now safely lodged in perfect bliss; and with spirits elated to rapture, with Henry at her heart, and Northanger Abbey on her lips, she hurried home to write her letter.

NA

Emulation

Nothing was fixed on; but Henry Crawford was full of ideas and projects, and, generally speaking, whatever he proposed was immediately approved, first by her, and then by Mr. Rushworth, whose principal business seemed to be to hear the others, and who scarcely risked an original thought of his own beyond a wish that they had seen his friend Smith's place.

MP

England

It was a sweet view—sweet to the eye and the mind. English verdure, English culture, English comfort, seen under a sun bright, without being oppressive.

EM

"Remember the country and the age in which we live. Remember that we are English, that we are Christians. Consult your own understanding, your own sense of the probable, your own observation of what is passing around you. Does our education prepare us for such atrocities? Do our laws connive at them? Could they be perpetrated without being known, in a country like this, where social and literary intercourse is on such a footing, where every man is surrounded by a neighbourhood of voluntary spies, and where roads and newspapers lay everything open?"
Henry Tilney, NA

I hope your letters from abroad are satisfactory. They would not be satisfactory to *me*, I confess, unless they breathed a strong spirit of regret for not being in England.
JAL

This woman had the good luck of being advanced to the throne of England, in spite of the superior pretensions, Merit, and Beauty of her Cousins Mary Queen of Scotland and Jane Grey. Nor can I pity the Kingdom for the misfortunes they experienced during her reign since they fully deserved them for having allowed her to succeed her brother.
JU

Entertaining

A private dance, without sitting down to supper, was pronounced an infamous fraud upon the rights of men and women; and Mrs. Weston must not speak of it again.
EM

Excitement

These were thrilling words, and wound up Catherine's feelings to the highest point of ecstasy. Her grateful and gratified heart could hardly restrain its expressions within the language of tolerable calmness. To receive so flattering an invitation! To have her company so warmly solicited! Everything honourable and soothing, every present enjoyment, and every future hope was contained in it.
NA

Eyes

". . . the very great pleasure which a pair of fine eyes in the face of a pretty woman can bestow."
Fitzwilliam Darcy, PP

Fainting

A young lady who faints, must be recovered; questions must be answered, and surprizes be explained. Such events are very interesting, but the suspense of them cannot last long.
EM

Never did I see such an affecting Scene as was the meeting of Edward and Augustus. "My Life! my Soul!" exclaimed the former.

"My Adorable Angel!" replied the latter, as they flew into each other's arms. It was too pathetic for the feelings of Sophia and myself—We fainted alternately on a sofa.
LF

Faithlessness

"If such is your way of thinking," said Marianne, "if the loss of what is most valued is so easily to be made up by something else, your resolution, your self-command, are, perhaps, a little less to be wondered at.—They are brought more within my comprehension."
Marianne Dashwood, SS

Falling from Grace

She must withdraw . . . to a retirement and reproach which could allow no second spring of hope or character.
MP

Falling in Love

His society became gradually her most exquisite enjoyment. They read, they talked, they sang together; his musical talents were considerable; and he read with all the sensibility and spirit which Edward had unfortunately wanted.
SS

But no sooner had he made it clear to himself and his friends that she had hardly a good feature in her face, than he began to find it was rendered uncommonly intelligent by the beautiful expression of her dark eyes. To this discovery succeeded some others equally mortifying. Though he had detected with a critical eye more than one failure of perfect symmetry in her form, he was forced to acknowledge her figure to be light and pleasing; and in spite of his asserting that her manners were not those of the fashionable world, he was caught by their easy playfulness. Of this she was

perfectly unaware;—to her he was only the man who made himself agreeable no where, and who had not thought her handsome enough to dance with. He began to wish to know more of her, and as a step towards conversing with her himself, attended to her conversation with others.
PP

Elizabeth . . . wanted Mr. Darcy to account for his having ever fallen in love with her. "How could you begin?" said she. "I can comprehend your going on charmingly, when you had once made a beginning, but what could set you off in the first place?"

"I cannot fix on the hour, or the spot, or the look, or the words, which laid the foundation. It is too long ago. I was in the middle before I knew that I *had* begun."
Elizabeth Bennet, Fitzwilliam Darcy, PP

She began now to comprehend that he was exactly the man who, in disposition and talents, would most suit her. His understanding and temper, though unlike her own, would have answered all her wishes. It was an union that must have been to the advantage of both; by her ease and liveliness, his mind might have been softened, his manners improved, and from his judgment, information, and knowledge of the world, she must have received benefit of greater importance.
PP

Family

Children of the same family, the same blood, with the same first associations and habits, have some means of enjoyment in their power, which no subsequent connections can supply; and it must be by a long and unnatural estrangement, by a divorce which no subsequent connection can

justify, if such precious remains of the earliest attachments are ever entirely outlived.
MP

Family and courtship

There is scarcely a young lady in the united kingdoms, who would not rather put up with the misfortune of being sought by a clever, agreeable man, than have him driven away by the vulgarity of her nearest relations.
MP

Family embarrassments

To Elizabeth it appeared, that had her family made an agreement to expose themselves as much as they could during the evening, it would have been impossible for them to play their parts with more spirit, or finer success.
PP

. . . the mother was found to be intolerable, and the younger sisters not worth speaking to . . .
PP

Family heritage

My father was a native of Ireland and an inhabitant of Wales; my mother was the natural daughter of a Scotch peer by an Italian Opera girl—I was born in Spain and received my education at a convent in France.
LF

Family planning

I would recommend to her and Mr. D. the simple regimen
of separate rooms [to prevent conception].
JAL

Poor woman! how can she honestly be breeding again?
JAL

Family quarrels

"Family squabbling is the greatest evil of all, and we had
better do any thing than be altogether by the ears."
Edmund Bertram, MP

Family relationships

The comfort, the freedom, the gaiety of the room was over,
hushed into cold composure, determined silence, or insipid
talk, to meet the heartless elegance of her father and sister.
How mortifying to feel that it was so!
PER

Fashion

I learnt from Mrs. Tickars's young lady, to my high amusement, that the stays now are not made to force the bosom
up at all; that was a very unbecoming, unNatural fashion.
JAL

Fashion—men and women

For man only can be aware of the insensibility of man towards a new gown. It would be mortifying to the feelings of many ladies, could they be made to understand how little the heart of man is affected by what is costly or new in their attire; how little it is biased by the texture of their muslin, and how unsusceptible of peculiar tenderness towards the spotted, the sprigged, the mull, or the jackonet. Woman is fine for her own satisfaction alone. No man will admire her the more, no woman will like her the better for it. Neatness and fashion are enough for the former, and a something of shabbiness or impropriety will be most endearing to the latter.

NA

Fathers

It was a melancholy change; and Emma could not but sigh over it, and wish for impossible things, till her father awoke, and made it necessary to be cheerful.

EM

She dearly loved her father, but he was no companion for her. He could not meet her in conversation, rational or playful.

EM

They were interrupted by Miss Bennet, who came to fetch her mother's tea. "This is a parade," cried he, "which does one good; it gives such an elegance to misfortune! Another day I will do the same; I will sit in my library, in my night cap and powdering gown, and give as much trouble as I can."

Mr. Bennet, PP

When Mr. Bennet arrived, he had all the appearance of his usual philosophic composure. He said as little as he had ever been in the habit of saying; made no mention of the business that had taken him away, and it was some time before his daughters had courage to speak of it.
PP

He had known many disagreeable fathers before, and often been struck with the inconveniences they occasioned, but never, in the whole course of his life, had he seen one of that class so unintelligibly moral, so infamously tyrannical as Sir Thomas.
MP

Fathers and daughters

"I am not going to run away, Papa," said Kitty fretfully; "if I should ever go to Brighton I would behave better than Lydia."

"You go to Brighton—I would not trust you so near it as East-Bourne, for fifty pounds! No, Kitty, I have at last learnt to be cautious, and you will feel the effects of it. No officer is ever to enter my house again, nor even to pass through the village. Balls will be absolutely prohibited, unless you stand up with one of your sisters. And you are never to stir out of doors till you can prove that you have spent ten minutes of every day in a rational manner."

Kitty, who took all these threats in a serious light, began to cry.

"Well, well," said he, "do not make yourself unhappy. If you are a good girl for the next ten years, I will take you to a review at the end of them."
Kitty Bennet, Mr. Bennet, PP

First Impressions

He set off directly for the cottage to tell the Miss Dashwoods of the Miss Steeles' arrival, and to assure them of their being the sweetest girls in the world. From such commendation as this, however, there was not much to be learned; Elinor well knew that the sweetest girls in the world were to be met with in every part of England, under every possible variation of form, face, temper and understanding.
SS

"He is very handsome indeed."
"Handsome! Yes, I suppose he may. I dare say people would admire him in general; but he is not at all in my style of beauty. I hate a florid complexion and dark eyes in a man. However, he is very well. Amazingly conceited, I am sure."
Catherine Morland, Isabella Thorpe, NA

Flattery

Where youth and diffidence are united, it requires uncommon steadiness of reason to resist the attraction of being called the most charming girl in the world.
NA

Their manners were particularly civil, and Elinor soon allowed them credit for some kind of sense, when she saw with what constant and judicious attention they were making themselves agreeable to Lady Middleton. With her children they were in continual raptures, extolling their beauty, courting their notice, and humouring their whims; and such of their time as could be spared from the importunate demands which this politeness made on it, was spent in ad-

miration of whatever her ladyship was doing, if she happened to be doing any thing, or in taking patterns of some elegant new dress, in which her appearance the day before had thrown them into unceasing delight.
SS

To flatter and follow others, without being flattered and followed in turn, is but a state of half enjoyment.
PER

"Can you trust me with such flatterers?—Does my vain spirit ever tell me I am wrong?"
Emma Woodhouse, EM

"Her ignorance is hourly flattery."
George Knightley, EM

Flirting

"I never in my life saw a man more intent on being agreeable than Mr. Elton. It is downright labour to him where ladies are concerned. With men he can be rational and unaffected, but when he has ladies to please, every feature works."
George Knightley, EM

"I see what you think of me," said he gravely—"I shall make but a poor figure in your journal tomorrow."
    "My journal!"
    "Yes, I know exactly what you will say: Friday, went to the Lower Rooms; wore my sprigged muslin robe with blue trimmings—plain black shoes—appeared to much advantage; but was strangely harassed by a queer, half-witted man, who would make me dance with him, and distressed me by his nonsense."

"Indeed I shall say no such thing."

"Shall I tell you what you ought to say?"

"If you please."

"I danced with a very agreeable young man, introduced by Mr. King; had a great deal of conversation with him—seems a most extraordinary genius—hope I may know more of him. *That*, madam, is what I *wish* you to say."

"But, perhaps, I keep no journal."

"Perhaps you are not sitting in this room, and I am not sitting by you. These are points in which a doubt is equally possible.

Henry Tilney, Catherine Morland, NA

Every distinguishing attention that could be paid, was paid to her. To amuse her, and be agreeable in her eyes, seemed all that he cared for—and Emma, glad to be enlivened, not sorry to be flattered, was gay and easy too, and gave him all the friendly encouragement, the admission to be gallant, which she had ever given in the first and most animating period of their acquaintance.

EM

There had been no real affection either in his language or manners. Sighs and fine words had been given in abundance; but she could hardly devise any set of expressions, or fancy any tone of voice, less allied with real love. She need not trouble herself to pity him. He only wanted to aggrandise and enrich himself.

EM

"But if a woman is partial to a man, and does not endeavour to conceal it, he must find it out."

"Perhaps he must, if he sees enough of her. But though Bingley and Jane meet tolerably often, it is never for many hours together; and as they always see each other in large mixed parties, it is impossible that every moment should be

employed in conversing together. Jane should therefore make the most of every half hour in which she can command his attention. When she is secure of him, there will be leisure for falling in love as much as she chuses."
Elizabeth Bennet, Charlotte Lucas, PP

Flirting and love

"I understand: she is in love with James, and flirts with Frederick."

"Oh! no, not flirts. A woman in love with one man cannot flirt with another."

"It is probable that she will neither love so well, nor flirt so well, as she might do either singly. The gentlemen must each give up a little."
Henry Tilney, Catherine Morland, NA

Flowers and Love

"I have just learned to love a hyacinth."

"And how might you learn?—By accident or argument?"

"Your sister taught me; I cannot tell how. Mrs. Allen used to take pains, year after year, to make me like them, but I never could, till I saw them the other day in Milsom Street; I am Naturally indifferent about flowers."

"But now you love a hyacinth. So much the better. You have gained a new source of enjoyment, and it is well to have as many holds upon happiness as possible. Besides, a taste for flowers is always desirable in your sex, as a means of getting you out of doors, and tempting you to more frequent exercise than you would otherwise take. And though the love of a hyacinth may be rather domestic, who can tell, the sentiment once raised, but you may in time come to love a rose?"
Catherine Morland, Henry Tilney, NA

Folly

"I do not know whether it ought to be so, but certainly silly things do cease to be silly if they are done by sensible people in an impudent way. Wickedness is always wickedness, but folly is not always folly.—It depends upon the character of those who handle it.
Emma Woodhouse, EM

"How despicably have I acted!" she cried. "I, who have prided myself on my discernment!—I, who have valued myself on my abilities! . . . How humiliating is this discovery!—Yet, how just a humiliation!—Had I been in love, I could not have been more wretchedly blind, but vanity, not love, has been my folly.—Pleased with the preference of one, and offended by the neglect of the other, on the very beginning of our acquaintance, I have courted prepossession and ignorance, and driven reason away, where either were concerned. Till this moment, I never knew myself."
Elizabeth Bennet, PP

Foolishness

"She is not a sensible girl, nor a girl of any information. She has been taught nothing useful, and is too young and too simple to have acquired any thing herself. At her age she can have no experience, and with her little wit, is not very likely ever to have any that can avail her. She is pretty, and she is good tempered, and that is all."
George Knightley, EM

Foppishness

After this speech he was gone as soon as possible. Emma could not think it too soon; for with all his good and agree-

able qualities, there was a sort of parade in his speeches
which was very apt to incline her to laugh.
EM

Fortitude

Altho' I cannot agree with you in supposing that I shall
never again be exposed to Misfortunes as unmerited as
those I have already experienced, yet to avoid the imputa-
tion of Obstinacy or ill-nature, I will gratify the curiosity of
your Daughter; and may the fortitude with which I have
suffered the many afflictions of my past Life, prove to her a
useful lesson for the support of those which may befall her
in her own.
LF

Frankness

"But disguise of every sort is my abhorrence."
Fitzwilliam Darcy, PP

She prized the frank, the open-hearted, the eager character
beyond all others. Warmth and enthusiasm did captivate
her still. She felt that she could so much more depend upon
the sincerity of those who sometimes looked or said a careless or a hasty thing, than of those whose presence of mind
never varied, whose tongue never slipped.
PER

Freckles

". . . That tooth of hers and those freckles. Freckles do not
disgust me so very much as they do him. I have known a

face not materially disfigured by a few, but he abominates them. You must have heard him notice Mrs. Clay's freckles."
Elizabeth Elliot, PER

Friendship

Friendship is certainly the finest balm for the pangs of disappointed love.
NA

She had been a friend and companion such as few possessed: intelligent, well-informed, useful, gentle, knowing all the ways of the family, interested in all its concerns, and peculiarly interested in herself, in every pleasure, every scheme of hers—one to whom she could speak every thought as it arose, and who had such an affection for her as could never find fault.
EM

The progress of the friendship between Catherine and Isabella was quick as its beginning had been warm, and they passed so rapidly through every gradation of increasing tenderness that there was shortly no fresh proof of it to be given to their friends or themselves. They called each other by their Christian Name, were always arm in arm when they walked, pinned up each other's train for the dance, and were not to be divided in the set . . .
NA

Their conversation turned upon those subjects, of which the free discussion has generally much to do in perfecting a sudden intimacy between two young ladies: such as dress, balls, flirtations, and quizzes. Miss Thorpe, however, being four years older than Miss Morland, and at least four years better informed, had a very decided advantage in discussing such points; she could compare the balls of Bath with those of Tunbridge, its fashions with the fashions of London; could rectify the opinions of her new friend in many articles of tasteful attire; could discover a flirtation between any gentleman and lady who only smiled on each other; and point out a quiz through the thickness of a crowd.

NA

There was not a creature in the world to whom she spoke with such unreserve . . . not any one, to whom she related with such conviction of being listened to and understood, of being always interesting and always intelligible, the little affairs, arrangements, perplexities, and pleasures of her father and herself.

EM

Their good friend saw that Marianne was unhappy, and felt that every thing was due to her which might make her at all less so. She treated her therefore, with all the indulgent fondness of a parent towards a favourite child on the last day of its holidays. Marianne was to have the best place by the fire, was to be tempted to eat by every delicacy in the house, and to be amused by the relation of all the news of the day.

SS

"There is nothing I would not do for those who are really my friends. I have no notion of loving people by halves; it is not my Nature. My attachments are always excessively strong. I told Captain Hunt at one of our assemblies this winter that if he was to tease me all night, I would not dance with him, unless he would allow Miss Andrews to be as beautiful as an angel. The men think us incapable of real friendship, you know, and I am determined to show them the difference."

Isabella Thorpe, NA

Gardening

I will not say that your mulberry-trees are dead, but I am afraid they are not alive.
JAL

Gardens

They insensibly followed one another to the delicious shade of a broad short avenue of limes, which stretching beyond the garden at an equal distance from the river, seemed the finish of the pleasure grounds.—It led to nothing; nothing but a view at the end over a low stone wall with high pillars, which seemed intended, in their erection, to give the appearance of an approach to the house, which never had been there. Disputable, however, as might be the taste of such a termination, it was in itself a charming walk, and the view which closed it extremely pretty.
EM

Mr. Collins invited them to take a stroll in the garden, which was large and well laid out, and to the cultivation of which he attended himself. To work in his garden was one of his most respectable pleasures; . . . Here, leading the way through every walk and cross walk, and scarcely allowing them an interval to utter the praises he asked for, every view was pointed out with a minuteness which left beauty entirely behind. He could number the fields in every direction, and could tell how many trees there were in the most distant clump. But of all the views which his garden, or which the country, or the kingdom could boast, none were to be compared with the prospect of Rosings, afforded by an opening in the trees that bordered the park nearly opposite the front of his house.
PP

Gift Giving

You are very kind in planning presents for me to make, and my mother has shown me exactly the same attention; but as I do not choose to have generosity dictated to me, I shall not resolve on giving my cabinet to Anna till the first thought of it has been my own.
JAL

Giving In

Elinor agreed to it all, for she did not think he deserved the compliment of rational opposition.
SS

Good Company

"My idea of good company, Mr. Elliot, is the company of clever, well-informed people, who have a great deal of conversation; that is what I call good company."

"You are mistaken," said he gently, "that is not good company; that is the best. Good company requires only birth, education, and manners, and with regard to education is not very nice. Birth and good manners are essential; but a little learning is by no means a dangerous thing in good company; on the contrary, it will do very well."
Anne Elliot, Mr. Elliot, PER

"Nobody cares for a letter; the thing is, to be always happy with pleasant companions."
Harriet Smith, EM

And they are each of them so agreeable in their different way, and harmonise so well, that their visit is thorough enjoyment.
JAL

Gossip

"You will have a great deal of unreserved discourse with Mrs. K., I dare say, upon this subject, as well as upon many other of our family matters. Abuse everybody but me."
JAL

As to the sad catastrophe itself, it could be canvassed only in one style by a couple of steady, sensible women, whose judgements had to work on ascertained events; and it was perfectly decided that it had been the consequence of much thoughtlessness and much imprudence; that its effects were most alarming, and that it was frightful to think, how long Miss Musgrove's recovery might yet be doubtful, and how liable she would still remain to suffer from the concussion hereafter!
PER

Her manners were pronounced to be very bad indeed, a mixture of pride and impertinence; she had no conversation, no stile, no taste, no beauty. Mrs. Hurst thought the same, and added, "She has nothing, in short, to recommend her, but being an excellent walker. I shall never forget her appearance this morning. She really looked almost wild."
Mrs. Hurst, PP

"I do not require you to adopt all my suspicions, though you make so noble a profession of doing it, but I honestly tell you what they are."
Emma Woodhouse, EM

"The truth is, that our inquiries were too direct; we sent a servant, we went ourselves: this will not do seventy miles from London; but this morning we heard of it in the right way. It was seen by some farmer, and he told the miller, and the miller told the butcher, and the butcher's son-in-law left word at the shop."
Mary Crawford, MP

She wished very much to have the subject continued, though she did not chuse to join in it herself; but nothing more of it was said, and for the first time in her life, she thought Mrs. Jennings deficient either in curiosity after petty information, or in a disposition to communicate it. The manner in which Miss Steele had spoken of Edward, increased her curiosity; for it struck her as being rather ill-natured, and suggested the suspicion of that lady's knowing, or fancying herself to know something to his disadvantage.
SS

Unluckily however, I see nothing to be glad of, unless I make it a matter of Joy that Mrs. Wylmot has another son, & that Lord Lucan has taken a Mistress, both of which Events are of course joyful to the Actors [i.e., participants].
JAL

Grudge Holding

"My temper I dare not vouch for.—It is I believe too little yielding—certainly too little for the convenience of the world. I cannot forget the follies and vices of others so soon as I ought, nor their offences against myself. My feelings are not puffed about with every attempt to move them. My temper would perhaps be called resentful.—My good opinion once lost is lost for ever."
Fitzwilliam Darcy, PP

Guilt

"It has been my own doing, and I ought to feel it."
   "You must not be too severe upon yourself," replied Elizabeth.
   "You may well warn me against such an evil. Human Nature is so prone to fall into it!"
Mr. Bennet, Elizabeth Bennet, PP

Habit

"Oh, the difference of situation and habit!"
Emma Woodhouse, EM

Happiness

. . . all those little matters on which the daily happiness of private life depends.
EM

"I assure you the utmost stretch of public fame would not make me amends for the loss of any happiness in private life."
Mr. Weston, EM

"How often is happiness destroyed by preparation, foolish preparation!"
Frank Churchill, EM

Perfect happiness, even in memory, is not common.
EM

She was in dancing, singing, exclaiming spirits; and till she had moved about, and talked to herself, and laughed and reflected, she could be fit for nothing rational.
EM

Happy Endings

A heroine returning, at the close of her career, to her native village, in all the triumph of recovered reputation, and all the dignity of a countess, with a long train of noble relations in their several phaetons, and three waiting-maids in a travelling chaise and four, behind her, is an event on which the

pen of the contriver may well delight to dwell; it gives credit to every conclusion, and the author must share in the glory she so liberally bestows.
NA

Hats

Next week [I] shall begin my operations on my hat, on which you know my principal hopes of happiness depend.
JAL

I can't help thinking that it is more Natural to have flowers grow out of the head than fruit. What do you think on that subject?
JAL

Having Fun

I had a very pleasant evening, however, though you will probably find out that there was no particular reason for it; but I do not think it worth while to wait for enjoyment until there is some real opportunity for it.
JAL

Healing

Every thing that the most zealous affection, the most solici-tous care could do to render her comfortable, was the office of each watchful companion, and each found their reward in her bodily ease, and her calmness of spirits. To Elinor, the observation of the latter was particularly grateful. She, who had seen her week after week so constantly suffering, op-pressed by anguish of heart which she had neither courage

to speak of, nor fortitude to conceal, now saw with a joy, which no other could equally share, an apparent composure of mind, which, in being the result as she trusted of serious reflection, must eventually lead her to contentment and cheerfulness.
SS

Healing Power of Time

What might not eight years do? Events of every description, changes, alienations, removals—all, all must be comprised in it, and oblivion of the past—how Natural, how certain too!
PER

Health

"As to myself, I have been long perfectly convinced, though perhaps I never told you so before, that the sea is very rarely of use to any body. I am sure it almost killed me once."
Mr. Woodhouse, EM

Dangers to health

"Ah! my dear, as Perry says, where health is at stake, nothing else should be considered; and if one is to travel, there is not much to chuse between forty miles and an hundred.— Better not move at all, better stay in London altogether than travel forty miles to get into a worse air."
Mr. Woodhouse, EM

"It is very pretty," said Mr. Woodhouse. "So prettily done! Just as your drawings always are, my dear. I do not know any body who draws so well as you do. The only thing I do not thoroughly like is, that she seems to be sitting out of doors, with only a little shawl over her shoulders—and it makes one think she must catch cold."

"But, my dear papa, it is supposed to be summer; a warm day in summer. Look at the tree."

"But it is never safe to sit out of doors, my dear."
Mr. Woodhouse, Emma Woodhouse, EM

"It was an awkward business, my dear, your spending the autumn at South End instead of coming here. I never had much opinion of the sea air."
Mr. Woodhouse, EM

Gruel and health

"You and I will have a nice basin of gruel together. My dear Emma, suppose we all have a little gruel." Emma could not suppose any such thing, knowing as she did, that both the Mr. Knightleys were as unpersuadable on that article as herself;—and two basins only were ordered. After a little more discourse in praise of gruel, with some wondering at its not being taken every evening by every body.
Mr. Woodhouse, EM

Heroines

A heroine in a hack post-chaise is such a blow upon sentiment, as no attempt at grandeur or pathos can withstand.
NA

To be disgraced in the eye of the world, to wear the appearance of infamy while her heart is all purity, her actions all innocence, and the misconduct of another the true source of

her debasement, is one of those circumstances which peculiarly belong to the heroine's life, and her fortitude under it what particularly dignifies her character.
NA

When a young lady is to be a heroine, the perverseness of forty surrounding families cannot prevent her. Something must and will happen to throw a hero in her way.
NA

History

"Yes, I am fond of history."

"I wish I were too. I read it a little as a duty, but it tells me nothing that does not either vex or weary me. The quarrels of popes and kings, with wars or pestilences, in every page; the men all so good for nothing, and hardly any women at all—it is very tiresome: and yet I often think it odd that it should be so dull, for a great deal of it must be invention. The speeches that are put into the heroes' mouths, their thoughts and designs—the chief of all this must be invention, and invention is what delights me in other books."
Eleanor Tilney, Catherine Morland, NA

Home

They were wise enough to be contented with the house as it was; and each of them was busy in arranging their particular concerns, and endeavoring, by placing around them books and other possessions, to form themselves a home.
SS

"There is nothing like staying at home for real comfort."
Mrs. Elton, EM

Hope

"Know your own happiness. You want nothing but patience—or give it a more fascinating Name, call it hope."
Mrs. Dashwood, SS

Hopelessness

[Elinor] could not witness the rapture of delightful expectation which filled the whole soul and beamed in the eyes of Marianne, without feeling how blank was her own prospect, how cheerless her own state of mind in the comparison, and how gladly she would engage in the solicitude of Marianne's situation to have the same animating object in view, the same possibility of hope.
SS

Human Nature

Nobody ever feels or acts or suffers or enjoys, as one expects.
JAL

Human Nature is so well disposed towards those who are in interesting situations, that a young person, who either marries or dies, is sure of being kindly spoken of.
EM

"It is very difficult for the prosperous to be humble."
Frank Churchill, EM

Seldom, very seldom, does complete truth belong to any human disclosure; seldom can it happen that something is not a little disguised, or a little mistaken.
EM

The power of disappointing them, it was true, must always be her's. But that was not enough; for when people are determined on a mode of conduct which they know to be wrong, they feel injured by the expectation of any thing better from them.
SS

There are people, who the more you do for them, the less they will do for themselves.
EM

Humility

"Nothing is more deceitful," said Darcy, "than the appearance of humility. It is often only carelessness of opinion, and sometimes an indirect boast."
Fitzwilliam Darcy, PP

Husbands and Wives

Husbands and wives generally understand when opposition will be vain.
PER

Mr. Bennet was so odd a mixture of quick parts, sarcastic humour, reserve, and caprice, that the experience of three and twenty years had been insufficient to make his wife understand his character. *Her* mind was less difficult to develope. She was a woman of mean understanding, little information, and uncertain temper. When she was discontented, she fancied herself nervous. The business of her life was to get her daughters married; its solace was visiting and news.
PP

Mrs. Hall, of Sherborne, was brought to bed yesterday of a dead child, some weeks before she was expected, owing to a fright. I suppose that she happened unawares to look at her husband.
JAL

Her husband, however, would not agree with her here; for . . . his cousin Charles Hayter was an eldest son, and he saw things as an eldest son himself.
PER

Hypochondria

"I am sorry to hear you say so, sir; but I assure you, excepting those little nervous head-aches and palpitations which I am never entirely free from anywhere, I am quite well myself."
Isabella Knightley, EM

Hypocrisy

Like many other great moralists and preachers, she had been eloquent on a point in which her own conduct would ill bear examination.
PER

Hysteria

"Tell him what a dreadful state I am in, that I am frighted out of my wits—and have such tremblings, such flutterings, all over me—such spasms in my side and pains in my head, and such beatings at heart, that I can get no rest by night nor by day."
Mrs. Bennet, PP

Avoiding hysteria

Instead of turning of a deathlike paleness and falling in a fit on Mrs. Allen's bosom, Catherine sat erect, in the perfect use of her senses, and with cheeks only a little redder than usual.
NA

Idleness

I have read [Byron's] The Corsair, mended my petticoat, and have nothing else to do.
JAL

"A man who has nothing to do with his own time has no conscience in his intrusion on that of others."
Marianne Dashwood, SS

Ignorance

Lucy was Naturally clever; her remarks were often just and amusing; and as a companion for half an hour Elinor frequently found her agreeable; but her powers had received no aid from education: she was ignorant and illiterate; and her deficiency of all mental improvement, her want of information in the most common particulars, could not be concealed from Miss Dashwood, in spite of her constant endeavour to appear to advantage.
SS

Imbecility in females is a great enhancement of their personal charms.
NA

Ill Disposition

He was not an ill-disposed young man, unless to be rather cold hearted and rather selfish is to be ill-disposed.
SS

Ill Nature

Mrs. Ferrars was a little, thin woman, upright, even to formality, in her figure, and serious, even to sourness, in her aspect. Her complexion was sallow; and her features small, without beauty, and Naturally without expression; but a lucky contraction of the brow had rescued her countenance from the disgrace of insipidity, by giving it the strong characters of pride and ill Nature.
SS

Illness

My attendant is encouraging, and talks of making me quite well. I live chiefly on the sofa, but am allowed to walk from one room to the other. I have been out once in a sedan-chair, and am to repeat it, and be promoted to a wheel-chair as the weather serves.
JAL

She then went away, walking on tiptoe out of the room, as if she supposed her young friend's affliction could be increased by noise.
SS

Illness and fortitude

What instances must pass before them of ardent, disinterested, self-denying attachment, of heroism, fortitude, patience, resignation—of all the conflicts and the sacrifices that ennoble us most. A sick room may often furnish the worth of volumes.
PER

Illness and human nature

"Here and there, human Nature may be great in times of trial, but generally speaking it is its weakness and not its strength that appears in a sick chamber."
Mrs. Smith, PER

Imagination

A mind lively and at ease, can do with seeing nothing, and can see nothing that does not answer.
EM

You express so little anxiety about my being murdered under Ash Park Copse by Mrs. Hulbert's servant, that I have a great mind not to tell you whether I was or not.
JAL

Pretensions to judgment

She walked on, amusing herself in the consideration of the blunders which often arise from a partial knowledge of circumstances, of the mistakes which people of high pretensions to judgment are for ever falling into.
EM

Imperfection (in praise of)

He and I should not in the least agree, of course, in our ideas of novels and heroines. Pictures of perfection, as you know, make me sick and wicked.
JAL

Importance

"Importance may sometimes be purchased too dearly."
Elizabeth Bennet, PP

Impressions

"Very odd! but one never does form a just idea of any body beforehand. One takes up a notion, and runs away with it."
Jane Bates, EM

Her early impressions were incurable.
PER

"Engagement!" cried Marianne, "there has been no engagement."
  "No engagement!"
  "No, he is not so unworthy as you believe him. He has broken no faith with me."
  "But he told you that he loved you."
  "Yes—no—never absolutely. It was every day implied, but never professedly declared. Sometimes I thought it had been—but it never was."
—Marianne Dashwood, Elinor Dashwood, SS

"I do not want to think ill of him. I should be as ready to acknowledge his merits as any other man; but I hear of none,

except what are merely personal; that he is well-grown and good-looking, with smooth, plausible manners."
George Knightley, EM

Improvements

"Ay, you have been brought up to it. It was no part of my education; and the only dose I ever had, being administered by not the first favourite in the world, has made me consider improvements *in hand* as the greatest of nuisances. Three years ago the Admiral, my honoured uncle, bought a cottage at Twickenham for us all to spend our summers in; and my aunt and I went down to it quite in raptures; but it being excessively pretty, it was soon found necessary to be improved, and for three months we were all dirt and confusion, without a gravel walk to step on, or a bench fit for use. I would have everything as complete as possible in the country, shrubberies and flower-gardens, and rustic seats innumerable: but it must all be done without my care."
Mary Crawford, MP

"The air of a gentleman's residence, therefore, you cannot but give it, if you do anything. But it is capable of much more. . . . By some such improvements as I have suggested. . . . You may raise it into a *place*. From being the mere gentleman's residence, it becomes, by judicious improvement, the residence of a man of education, taste, modern manners, good connections."
Henry Crawford, MP

Income

Edward had two thousand pounds, and Elinor one, which, with Delaford living, was all that they could call their own;

for it was impossible that Mrs. Dashwood should advance anything; and they were neither of them quite enough in love to think that three hundred and fifty pounds a-year would supply them with the comforts of life.
SS

Independence

"I had thought you peculiarly free from wilfulness of temper, self-conceit, and every tendency to that independence of spirit which prevails so much in modern days, even in young women, and which in young women is offensive and disgusting beyond all common offence. But you have now shown me that you can be wilful and perverse; that you can and will decide for yourself, without any consideration or deference for those who have surely some right to guide you, without even asking their advice. You have shown yourself very, very different from anything that I had imagined."
Sir Thomas Bertram, MP

After having so nobly disentangled themselves from the shackles of Parental Authority, by a Clandestine Marriage, they were determined never to forfeit the good opinion they had gained in the World, in so doing, by accepting any proposals of reconciliation that might be offered them by their Fathers—to this farther tryal of their noble independence, however, they never were exposed.
LF

Infatuation

There was nothing to denote him unworthy of the distinguished honour which her imagination had given him; the honour, if not of being really in love with her, of being at least very near it, and saved only by her own indifference—(for still her resolution held of never marrying)—the honour, in short, of being marked out for her by all their joint acquaintance.

EM

Again was Catherine disappointed in her hope of re-seeing her partner. He was nowhere to be met with; every search for him was equally unsuccessful, in morning lounges or evening assemblies; neither at the upper nor lower rooms, at dressed or undressed balls, was he perceivable; nor among the walkers, the horsemen, or the curricle-drivers of the morning. His Name was not in the pump-room book, and curiosity could do no more. He must be gone from Bath. Yet he had not mentioned that his stay would be so short! This sort of mysteriousness, which is always so becoming in a hero, threw a fresh grace in Catherine's imagination around his person and manners, and increased her anxiety to know more of him.

NA

His person and air were equal to what her fancy had ever drawn for the hero of a favourite story; and in his carrying her into the house with so little previous formality, there was a rapidity of thought which particularly recommended the action to her. Every circumstance belonging to him was interesting. His Name was good, his residence was in their favourite village, and she soon found out that of all manly dresses a shooting-jacket was the most becoming. Her imagination was busy, her reflections were pleasant, and the pain of a sprained ankle was disregarded.

SS

Now, it so happened that in spite of Emma's resolution of never marrying, there was something in the Name, in the

idea of Mr. Frank Churchill, which always interested her. She had frequently thought—especially since his father's marriage with Miss Taylor—that if she were to marry, he was the very person to suit her in age, character and condition.
EM

The youthful infatuation of nineteen would Naturally blind him to every thing but her beauty and good Nature; but the four succeeding years—years, which if rationally spent, give such improvement to the understanding, must have opened his eyes to her defects of education, while the same period of time, spent on her side in inferior society and more frivolous pursuits, had perhaps robbed her of that simplicity which might once have given an interesting character to her beauty.
SS

Inflexibility

His spirits required support. He was a nervous man, easily depressed; fond of every body that he was used to, and hating to part with them; hating change of every kind. Matrimony, as the origin of change, was always disagreeable; and he was by no means yet reconciled to things.
EM

Inheritance

"So you are to be a clergyman, Mr. Bertram. This is rather a surprise to me."

"Why should it surprise you? You must suppose me designed for some profession, and might perceive that I am neither a lawyer, nor a soldier, nor a sailor."

"Very true; but, in short, it had not occurred to me. And you know there is generally an uncle or a grandfather to leave a fortune to the second son."

"A very praiseworthy practice," said Edmund, "but not quite universal. I am one of the exceptions, and *being* one, must do something for myself."

Mary Crawford, Edmund Bertram, MP

When we arrived at Edinburgh Sir Edward told me that as the Widow of his Son, he desired I would accept from his Hands of four Hundred a year. I graciously promised that I would, but could not help observing that the unsympathetic Baronet offered it more on account of my being the Widow of Edward than in being the refined and amiable Laura.

LF

Innocence

Ben and Anna walked here . . . and she looked so pretty, it was quite a pleasure to see her, so young and so blooming, and so innocent, as if she had never had a wicked thought in her life, which yet one has some reason to suppose she must have had, if we believe the doctrine of original sin.

JAL

Insincerity and Ignorance

She could have no lasting satisfaction in the company of a person who joined insincerity with ignorance.

SS

Insipidness

Elinor needed little observation to perceive that her reserve was a mere calmness of manner with which sense had nothing to do. Towards her husband and mother she was the same as to them; and intimacy was therefore neither to be looked for nor desired. She had nothing to say one day that she had not said the day before. Her insipidity was invariable, for even her spirits were always the same; and though she did not oppose the parties arranged by her husband, provided every thing were conducted in style and her two eldest children attended her, she never appeared to receive more enjoyment from them than she might have experienced in sitting at home;—and so little did her presence add to the pleasure of the others, by any share in their conversation, that they were sometimes only reminded of her being amongst them by her solicitude about her troublesome boys.
SS

Insult

"What a blessing, that she never had any children! Poor little creatures, how unhappy she would have made them!"
Isabella Knightley, EM

"SHE a beauty! I should as soon call her mother a wit."
Caroline Bingley, quoting Fitzwilliam Darcy to himself, PP

"A little upstart, vulgar being, with her Mr. E., and her caro sposo, and her resources, and all her airs of pert pretension and underbred finery."
Emma Woodhouse, EM

Integrity

She was a woman rather of sound than of quick abilities, whose difficulties in coming to any decision in this instance were great, from the opposition of two leading principles. She was of strict integrity herself, with a delicate sense of honour; but she was as desirous of saving Sir Walter's feelings, as solicitous for the credit of the family, as aristocratic in her ideas of what was due to them, as anybody of sense and honesty could well be.
PER

Intimacy

"It is not time or opportunity that is to determine intimacy; it is disposition alone. Seven years would be insufficient to make some people acquainted with each other, and seven days are more than enough for others."
Marianne Dashwood, SS

Jealousy

"It is Natural to suppose that we should be intimate,—that we should have taken to each other whenever she visited her friends. But we never did. I hardly know how it has happened; a little, perhaps, from that wickedness on my side which was prone to take disgust towards a girl so idolized and so cried up as she always was, by her aunt and grandmother, and all their set."
Emma Woodhouse, EM

She is in high favour with her Aunt altogether—because she is so little like myself, of course. She is exactly the com-

panion for Mrs. Vernon, who dearly loves to be first, & to
have all the sense & all the wit of the Conversation to herself: Frederica will never eclipse her.
LS

There was some satisfaction in considering with what self-
denying, generous friendship she had always wished and
promoted the match; but it was a black morning's work for
her.
EM

"I quite detest her. An odious, little, pert, unNatural, impudent girl. I have always protested against comedy, and this
is comedy in its worst form." And so saying, she walked
hastily out of the room, leaving awkward feelings to more
than one, but exciting small compassion in any except
Fanny, who had been a quiet auditor of the whole, and who
could not think of her as under the agitations of jealousy
without great pity.
Julia Bertram, MP

Jokes

"The wisest and the best of men, nay, the wisest and best of
their actions, may be rendered ridiculous by a person whose
first object in life is a joke."
Fitzwilliam Darcy, PP

Journal Writing

"Not keep a journal! How are your absent cousins to understand the tenour of your life in Bath without one? How are
the civilities and compliments of every day to be related as
they ought to be, unless noted down every evening in a

journal? How are your various dresses to be remembered, and the particular state of your complexion, and curl of your hair to be described in all their diversities, without having constant recourse to a journal? My dear madam, I am not so ignorant of young ladies' ways as you wish to believe me; it is this delightful habit of journaling which largely contributes to form the easy style of writing for which ladies are so generally celebrated."
Henry Tilney, NA

Judgment

"Better be without sense, than misapply it as you do."
George Knightley, EM

Letters

"The post-office has a great charm at one period of our lives. When you have lived to my age, you will begin to think letters are never worth going through the rain for."
John Knightley, EM

Letter writing

"Everybody allows that the talent of writing agreeable letters is peculiarly female. Nature may have done something, but I am sure it must be essentially assisted by the practice of keeping a journal."
Henry Tilney, NA

"He can sit down and write a fine flourishing letter, full of professions and falsehoods, and persuade himself that he has hit upon the very best method in the world of preserv-

ing peace at home and preventing his father's having any right to complain."
George Knightley, EM

I think it is time there should be a little writing between us, though I believe the epistolary debt is on *your* side, and I hope this will find all the Streatham party well, neither carried away by the flood, nor rheumatic through the damps.
JAL

"—how I have blushed over the pages of her writing!—and I believe I may say that since the first half year of our foolish—business—this is the only letter I ever received from her, of which the substance made me any amends for the defect of the style."
Edward Ferrars, SS

"If I write, I will say whatever you wish me; but I do not, at present, foresee any occasion for writing."

"No, I dare say, nor if he were to be gone a twelvemonth, would you ever write to him, nor he to you, if it could be helped. The occasion would never be foreseen. What strange creatures brothers are! You would not write to each other but upon the most urgent necessity in the world; and when obliged to take up the pen to say that such a horse is ill, or such a relation dead, it is done in the fewest possible words. You have but one style among you. I know it perfectly. Henry, who is in every other respect exactly what a brother should be, who loves me, consults me, confides in me, and will talk to me by the hour together, has never yet turned the page in a letter; and very often it is nothing more than—'Dear Mary, I am just arrived. Bath seems full, and everything as usual. Yours sincerely.' That is the true manly style; that is a complete brother's letter."
Edmund Bertram, Mary Crawford, MP

The style of the letter was much above her expectation. There were not merely no grammatical errors, but as a composition it would not have disgraced a gentleman; the language, though plain, was strong and unaffected, and the sentiments it conveyed very much to the credit of the writer. It was short, but expressed good sense, warm attachment, liberality, propriety, even delicacy of feeling.
EM

Life

Life seems but a quick succession of busy nothings.
JAL

London

I have also an idea of being soon in Town: & whatever may be my determination as to the rest, I shall probably put *that* project in execution—for London will always be the fairest field of action, however my views may be directed; & at any rate I shall there be rewarded by your society, & a little Dissipation.
LS

"*You* are speaking of London, *I* am speaking of the nation at large."
"The metropolis, I imagine, is a pretty fair sample of the rest."
"Not, I should hope, of the proportion of virtue to vice throughout the kingdom. We do not look in great cities for our best morality."
Edmund Bertram, Mary Crawford, MP

"Ah! my poor dear child, the truth is, that in London it is always a sickly season. Nobody is healthy in London, nobody can be. It is a dreadful thing to have you forced to live there! so far off!—and the air so bad!"
Mr. Woodhouse, EM

Here I am once more in this scene of dissipation and vice [London], and I begin already to find my morals corrupted.
JAL

Loneliness

The grandeur of the house astonished, but could not console her. The rooms were too large for her to move in with ease: whatever she touched she expected to injure, and she crept about in constant terror of something or other; often retreating towards her own chamber to cry; and the little girl who was spoken of in the drawing-room when she left it at night as seeming so desirably sensible of her peculiar good fortune, ended every day's sorrows by sobbing herself to sleep.
MP

Lost Love

This violent oppression of spirits continued the whole evening. She was without any power, because she was without any desire of command over herself. The slightest mention of anything relative to Willoughby overpowered her in an instant; and though her family were most anxiously attentive to her comfort, it was impossible for them, if they spoke at all, to keep clear of every subject which her feelings connected with him.
SS

"He will be forgot, and we shall all be as we were before."
Jane Bennet, PP

Never had she so honestly felt that she could have loved him, as now, when all love must be vain.
PP

"I shall do very well again after a little while—and then, it will be a good thing over; for they say every body is in love once in their lives, and I shall have been let off easily."
Emma Woodhouse, EM

Lost Youth

"I am sorry for that. At her time of life, any thing of an illness destroys the bloom for ever! Hers has been a very short one! She was as handsome a girl last September, as I ever saw; and as likely to attract the man. There was something in her style of beauty, to please them particularly."
John Dashwood, SS

Love

"She always declares she will never marry, which, of course, means just nothing at all. But I have no idea that she has yet ever seen a man she cared for. It would not be a bad thing for her to be very much in love with a proper object."
George Knightley, EM

"I must be in love; I should be the oddest creature in the world if I were not—for a few weeks at least."
Emma Woodhouse, EM

The lady had been so easily impressed—so sweetly disposed—had in short, to use a most intelligible phrase, been

so very ready to have him, that vanity and prudence were equally contented.
EM

What strength, or what constancy of affection he might be subject to, was another point; but at present she could not doubt his having a decidedly warm admiration, a conscious preference of herself; and this persuasion, joined to all the rest, made her think that she must be a little in love with him, in spite of every previous determination against it.
EM

"It does not often happen that the interference of friends will persuade a young man of independent fortune to think no more of a girl, whom he was violently in love with only a few days before.

"But that expression of 'violently in love' is so hackneyed, so doubtful, so indefinite, that it gives me very little idea. It is as often applied to feelings which arise from an half-hour's acquaintance, as to a real, strong attachment."
Elizabeth Bennet, Mrs. Gardiner, PP

From the moment of learning that Lucy was married to another, that Edward was free, to the moment of his justifying the hopes which had so instantly followed, she was every thing by turns but tranquil. But when the second moment had passed, when she found every doubt, every solicitude removed, compared her situation with what so lately it had been,—saw him honourably released from his former engagement, saw him instantly profiting by the release, to address herself and declare an affection as tender, as constant as she had ever supposed it to be,—she was oppressed, she was overcome by her own felicity;—and happily disposed as is the human mind to be easily familiarized with any change for the better, it required several hours to give se-

dateness to her spirits, or any degree of tranquillity to her heart.
SS

Prettier musings of high-wrought love and eternal constancy, could never have passed along the streets of Bath, than Anne was sporting with from Camden Place to Westgate Buildings. It was almost enough to spread purification and perfume all the way.
PER

... continual observation of, how much he seemed attached!—his air as he walked by the house—the very sitting of his hat, being all in proof of how much he was in love!
EM

Love and architecture

He could not believe it a bad house; not such a house as a man was to be pitied for having. If it were to be shared with the woman he loved, he could not think any man to be pitied for having that house. There must be ample room in it for every real comfort. The man must be a blockhead who wanted more.
EM

Love and constancy

"You pierce my soul. I am half agony, half hope. Tell me not that I am too late, that such precious feelings are gone for ever. I offer myself to you again with a heart even more your own than when you almost broke it, eight years and a half ago. Dare not say that man forgets sooner than woman, that his love has an earlier death. I have loved none but you. Unjust I may have been, weak and resentful I have been, but never inconstant. You alone have brought me to Bath. For you alone, I think and plan. Have you not seen this? Can you fail to have understood my wishes? I had not waited even these ten days, could I have read your feelings, as I think you must have penetrated mine. I can hardly write. I am every instant hearing something which over-powers me. You sink your voice, but I can distinguish the tones of that voice when they would be lost on others. Too good, too excellent creature! You do us justice, indeed. You do believe that there is true attachment and constancy among men. Believe it to be most fervent, most undeviat-ing, in F. W.

"I must go, uncertain of my fate; but I shall return hither, or follow your party, as soon as possible. A word, a look, will be enough to decide whether I enter your father's house this evening or never."
Frederick Wentworth, PER

Love and dining

"What a strange thing love is! he can see ready wit in Har-riet, but will not dine alone for her."
Emma Woodhouse, EM

Love and disappointment

Julia *did* suffer, however, though Mrs. Grant discerned it not, and though it escaped the notice of many of her own family likewise. She had loved, she did love still, and she had all the suffering which a warm temper and a high spirit were likely to endure under the disappointment of a dear, though irrational hope, with a strong sense of ill-usage. Her

heart was sore and angry, and she was capable only of angry consolations.
MP

Love and dreams

For if it be true, as a celebrated writer has maintained, that no young lady can be justified in falling in love before the gentleman's love is declared, it must be very improper that a young lady should dream of a gentleman before the gentleman is first known to have dreamt of her.
NA

Love and fate

"It is not every man's fate to marry the woman who loves him best."
Emma Woodhouse, EM

Love and fortune

"Do not involve yourself, or endeavour to involve him in an affection which the want of fortune would make so very imprudent."
Mrs. Gardiner, PP

Love and gallantry

"This man is almost too gallant to be in love," thought Emma. "I should say so, but that I suppose there may be a hundred different ways of being in love."
EM

Love and handwriting

The enthusiasm of a woman's love is even beyond the biographer's. To her, the handwriting itself, independent of anything it may convey, is a blessedness. Never were such characters cut by any other human being as Edmund's commonest handwriting gave! This specimen, written in haste as it was, had not a fault; and there was a felicity in the flow of the first four words, in the arrangement of "My very dear Fanny," which she could have looked at for ever.
MP

Love and marriage

"I have none of the usual inducements of women to marry. Were I to fall in love, indeed, it would be a different thing! but I never have been in love; it is not my way, or my Nature; and I do not think I ever shall. And, without love, I am sure I should be a fool to change such a situation as mine."
Emma Woodhouse, EM

Love and money

She was certainly not a woman of family, but well educated, accomplished, rich, and excessively in love with his friend. There had been the charm. . . . Here was a great deal to soften the business. A very fine woman with a large fortune, in love with him! Sir Walter seemed to admit it as complete apology; and though Elizabeth could not see the circumstance in quite so favourable a light, she allowed it be a great extenuation.
PER

Love and naïveté

She had talked her into love; but, alas! she was not so easily to be talked out of it. The charm of an object to occupy the many vacancies of Harriet's mind was not to be talked away.
EM

Love and poetry

However, he wrote some verses on her, and very pretty they were.

"And so ended his affection," said Elizabeth impatiently. "There has been many a one, I fancy, overcome in the same way. I wonder who first discovered the efficacy of poetry in driving away love!"

"I have been used to consider poetry as the food of love," said Darcy.

"Of a fine, stout, healthy love it may. Every thing nourishes what is strong already. But if it be only a slight, thin sort of inclination, I am convinced that one good sonnet will starve it entirely away."
Elizabeth Bennet, Fitzwilliam Darcy, PP

"Depend upon it, he would not like to have his charade slighted, much better than his passion. A poet in love must be encouraged in both capacities, or neither."
Emma Woodhouse, EM

Love and sentiment

As to any of that heroism of sentiment which might have prompted her to entreat him to transfer his affection from herself to Harriet, as infinitely the most worthy of the two—or even the more simple sublimity of resolving to refuse him at once and for ever, without vouchsafing any motive, because he could not marry them both—Emma had it not.
EM

Love at first sight

"So it always is with me; the first moment settles everything. The very first day that Morland came to us last Christmas—the very first moment I beheld him—my heart was irrecoverably gone. I remember I wore my yellow gown, with my hair done up in braids; and when I came into the drawing-room, and John introduced him, I thought I never saw anybody so handsome before." Here Catherine secretly acknowledged the power of love; for, though exceedingly fond of her brother, and partial to all his endowments, she had never in her life thought him handsome.
Isabella Thorpe, NA

Mary, without waiting for any further commands, immediately left the room and quickly returned, introducing the most beauteous and amiable Youth I had ever beheld. The servant, she kept to herself. My Natural sensibility had already been greatly affected by the sufferings of the unfortunate stranger and no sooner did I first behold him, than I felt that on him the happiness or Misery of my future Life must depend.
LF

Love letters

Such a letter was not to be soon recovered from. Half an hour's solitude and reflection might have tranquillized her; but the ten minutes only which now passed before she was interrupted, with all the restraints of her situation, could do nothing towards tranquillity. Every moment rather brought fresh agitation. It was overpowering happiness.
PER

Lovesickness

"He does sigh and languish, and study for compliments rather more than I could endure as a principal."
Emma Woodhouse, EM

A few months had seen the beginning and the end of their acquaintance; but not with a few months ended Anne's share of suffering from it. Her attachment and regrets had, for a long time, clouded every enjoyment of youth, and an early loss of bloom and spirits had been their lasting effect.
PER

Mr. Bennet treated the matter differently. "So, Lizzy," said he one day, "your sister is crossed in love I find. I congratulate her. Next to being married, a girl likes to be crossed in love a little now and then. It is something to think of, and gives her a sort of distinction among her companions. When is your turn to come? You will hardly bear to be long outdone by Jane. Now is your time. Here are officers enough at Meryton to disappoint all the young ladies in the country. Let Wickham be *your* man. He is a pleasant fellow, and would jilt you creditably."
Mr. Bennet, PP

She was humbled, she was grieved; she repented, though she hardly knew of what. She became jealous of his esteem, when she could no longer hope to be benefited by it. She wanted to hear of him, when there seemed the least chance of gaining intelligence. She was convinced that she would have been happy with him, when it was no longer likely that they should meet.
PP

Perfection of the beloved

... he had in fact nothing to dwell on but Fanny's charms. Fanny's beauty of face and figure, Fanny's graces of manner and goodness of heart, were the exhaustless theme. The gentleness, modesty, and sweetness of her character were warmly expatiated on; that sweetness which makes so essential a part of every woman's worth in the judgment of man, that though he sometimes loves where it is not, he can never believe it absent.
MP

Professions of love

What did she say?—Just what she ought, of course. A lady always does.—She said enough to show there need not be despair—and to invite him to say more himself.
EM

Symptoms of love

"I never saw a more promising inclination. He was growing quite inattentive to other people, and wholly engrossed by her. Every time they met, it was more decided and remarkable. At his own ball he offended two or three young ladies by not asking them to dance, and I spoke to him twice myself without receiving an answer. Could there be finer symptoms? Is not general incivility the very essence of love?"
Elizabeth Bennet, PP

Triumph in love

He had gone away rejected and mortified—disappointed in a very sanguine hope, after a series of what appeared to him strong encouragement; and not only losing the right lady, but finding himself debased to the level of a very wrong one. He had gone away deeply offended—he came back engaged to another—and to another as superior, of course, to the first, as under such circumstances what is gained always is to what is lost. He came back gay and self-satisfied, eager and busy, caring nothing for Miss Woodhouse, and defying Miss Smith.

EM

Let no one presume to give the feelings of a young woman on receiving the assurance of that affection of which she has scarcely allowed herself to entertain a hope.

MP

Love Thwarted

She laughed because she was disappointed; and though she liked him for his attentions, and thought them all, whether in friendship, admiration, or playfulness, extremely judicious, they were not winning back her heart. She still intended him for her friend.

EM

Loving in vain

That such letters, so full of affection and confidence, could have been so answered, Elinor, for Willoughby's sake, would have been unwilling to believe. But her condemnation of him did not blind her to the impropriety of their having been written at all; and she was silently grieving over the imprudence which had hazarded such unsolicited proofs of tenderness, not warranted by anything preceding, and most severely condemned by the event.

SS

Unrequited love

If it were love, it might be simple, single, successless love on her side alone.
EM

Lucky Guess

"And have you never known the pleasure and triumph of a lucky guess?—I pity you.—I thought you cleverer—for, depend upon it a lucky guess is never merely luck. There is always some talent in it.
Emma Woodhouse, EM

Madness

I am to meet Mrs. Harrison, and we are to talk about Ben and Anna."My dear Mrs. Harrison," I shall say,"I am afraid the young man has some of your family madness, and though there often appears to be something of madness in Anna too, I think she inherits more of it from her mother's family than from ours." That is what I shall say, and I think she will find it difficult to answer me.
JAL

Makeup

She was highly rouged, and looked rather quietly and contentedly silly than anything else.
JAL

Making Friends

She is really an agreeable girl, so I think I may like her; and her great want of a companion at home, which may well make any tolerable acquaintance important to her, gives her another claim on my attention. I shall endeavour as much as possible to keep my intimacies in their proper place, and prevent their clashing.
JAL

I do not want people to be very agreeable, as it saves me the trouble of liking them a great deal.
JAL

Manners

Elinor saw nothing to censure in him but a propensity, in which he strongly resembled and peculiarly delighted her sister, of saying too much what he thought on every occasion, without attention to persons or circumstances. In hastily forming and giving his opinion of other people, in sacrificing general politeness to the enjoyment of undivided attention where his heart was engaged, and in slighting too easily the forms of worldly propriety.
SS

Elinor had not needed this to be assured of the injustice to which her sister was often led in her opinion of others, by the irritable refinement of her own mind, and the too great importance placed by her on the delicacies of a strong sensibility, and the graces of a polished manner.
SS

You deserve a longer letter than this; but it is my unhappy fate seldom to treat people so well as they deserve.
JAL

"One man's style must not be the rule of another's."
George Knightley, EM

"Respect for right conduct is felt by every body."
George Knightley, EM

She found him, however, perfectly the gentleman in his behaviour to all his visitors, and only occasionally rude to his wife and her mother.
SS

Then, her understanding was beyond every suspicion, quick and clear; and her manners were the mirror of her own modest and elegant mind.
MP

Marriage

"A man would always wish to give a woman a better home than the one he takes her from."
George Knightley, EM

When any two young people take it into their heads to marry, they are pretty sure by perseverance to carry their point, be they ever so poor, or ever so imprudent, or ever so little likely to be necessary to each other's ultimate comfort.
PER

In all the important preparations of the mind she was complete: being prepared for matrimony by an hatred of home, restraint, and tranquillity; by the misery of disappointed affection, and contempt of the man she was to marry.
MP

Arranged marriage

If Maria could now speak so securely of her happiness with him, speaking certainly without the prejudice, the blindness of love, she ought to be believed. Her feelings, probably, were not acute; he had never supposed them to be so; but her comforts might not be less on that account; and if she could dispense with seeing her husband a leading, shining character, there would certainly be everything else in her favour. A well-disposed young woman, who did not marry for love, was in general but the more attached to her own family.
MP

Bad marriage

Had Elizabeth's opinion been all drawn from her own family, she could not have formed a very pleasing picture of conjugal felicity or domestic comfort. Her father, captivated by youth and beauty, and that appearance of good humour which youth and beauty generally give, had married a woman whose weak understanding and illiberal mind had, very early in their marriage, put an end to all real affection for her. Respect, esteem, and confidence had vanished for ever; and all his views of domestic happiness were overthrown.
PP

Distaste for marriage

Though always objecting to every marriage that was arranged, he never suffered beforehand from the apprehension of any; it seemed as if he could not think so ill of any two persons' understanding as to suppose they meant to marry till it were proved against them.
EM

Making a poor match

Miss Frances married, in the common phrase, to disoblige her family, and by fixing on a lieutenant of marines, without education, fortune, or connexions, did it very thoroughly. She could hardly have made a more untoward choice.
MP

Mrs. Allen was one of that numerous class of females, whose society can raise no other emotion than surprise at there being any men in the world who could like them well enough to marry them. She had neither beauty, genius, accomplishment, nor manner. The air of a gentlewoman, a great deal of quiet, inactive good temper, and a trifling turn of mind were all that could account for her being the choice of a sensible, intelligent man like Mr. Allen.
NA

Marriage advice

"This is an alliance which, whoever—whatever your friends may be, must be agreeable to them, provided at least they have common sense; and we are not to be addressing our conduct to fools. If they are anxious to see you happily married, here is a man whose amiable character gives every assurance of it;—if they wish to have you settled in the same country and circle which they have chosen to place you in, here it will be accomplished; and if their only object is that you should, in the common phrase, be well married, here is the comfortable fortune, the respectable establishment, the rise in the world which must satisfy them."
Emma Woodhouse, EM

Marriage and age

"Perhaps," said Elinor, "thirty-five and seventeen had better not have any thing to do with matrimony together. But if there should by any chance happen to be a woman who is single at seven and twenty, I should not think Colonel Brandon's being thirty-five any objection to his marrying HER."
Elinor Dashwood, SS

—a man . . . whom, two years before, she had considered too old to be married,—and who still sought the constitutional safeguard of a flannel waistcoat!
SS

Marriage and duty

". . . the very material matrimonial point of submitting your own will, and doing as you were bid."
George Knightley, EM

Marriage and fortune

It is a truth universally acknowledged, that a single man in possession of a good fortune must be in want of a wife. However little known the feelings or views of such a man may be on his first entering a neighbourhood, this truth is so well fixed in the minds of the surrounding families, that he is considered as the rightful property of some one or other of their daughters.
PP

About thirty years ago Miss Maria Ward, of Huntingdon, with only seven thousand pounds, had the good luck to cap-

tivate Sir Thomas Bertram, of Mansfield Park, in the county of Northampton, and to be thereby raised to the rank of a baronet's lady, with all the comforts and consequences of an handsome house and large income.
MP

Marriage and greed

"What is the difference in matrimonial affairs, between the mercenary and the prudent motive? Where does discretion end, and avarice begin?"
Elizabeth Bennet, PP

"I shall expect a new saddle horse, a suit of fine lace, and an infinite number of the most valuable jewels. Diamonds such as never were seen, (Pearls as large as those of the Princess Badroulbadour in the 4th volume of the Arabian Nights and rubies, emeralds, topazes, sapphires, amethysts, turkeystones, agates, beads, bugles, garnets) and pearls, rubies, emeralds, and beads out of number. You must set up your phaeton which must be cream coloured with a wreath of silver flowers round it, You must buy four of the finest bays in the kingdom and you must drive me in it every day. This is not all; you must entirely new furnish your house after my taste, you must hire two more footmen to attend me, two women to wait on me, must always let me do just as I please and make a very good husband." Here she stopped, I believe rather out of breath.
JU

Marriage and happiness

"Happiness in marriage is entirely a matter of chance. If the dispositions of the parties are ever so well known to each other, or ever so similar before-hand, it does not advance

their felicity in the least. They always contrive to grow sufficiently unlike afterwards to have their share of vexation; and it is better to know as little as possible of the defects of the person with whom you are to pass your life."
Charlotte Lucas, PP

Marriage and interfering parents

Henry and Catherine were married, the bells rang, and everybody smiled; and, as this took place within a twelvemonth from the first day of their meeting, it will not appear, after all the dreadful delays occasioned by the general's cruelty, that they were essentially hurt by it. To begin perfect happiness at the respective ages of twenty-six and eighteen is to do pretty well; and professing myself moreover convinced that the general's unjust interference, so far from being really injurious to their felicity, was perhaps rather conducive to it, by improving their knowledge of each other, and adding strength to their attachment, I leave it to be settled, by whomsoever it may concern, whether the tendency of this work be altogether to recommend parental tyranny, or reward filial disobedience.
NA

Marriage and respectability

Without thinking highly either of men or of matrimony, marriage had always been her object; it was the only honourable provision for well-educated young women of small fortune, and however uncertain of giving happiness, must be their pleasantest preservative from want. This preservative she had now obtained; and at the age of twenty-seven, without having ever been handsome, she felt all the good luck of it.
PP

Marriage ceremony

The wishes, the hopes, the confidence, the predictions of the small band of true friends who witnessed the ceremony, were fully answered in the perfect happiness of the union. EM

Marriage of convenience

"A woman of seven and twenty," said Marianne, after pausing a moment, "can never hope to feel or inspire affection again, and if her home be uncomfortable, or her fortune small, I can suppose that she might bring herself to submit to the offices of a nurse, for the sake of the provision and security of a wife. In his marrying such a woman therefore there would be nothing unsuitable. It would be a compact of convenience, and the world would be satisfied. In my eyes it would be no marriage at all, but that would be nothing. To me it would seem only a commercial exchange, in which each wished to be benefited at the expense of the other."
Marianne Dashwood, SS

"I am not romantic, you know. I never was. I ask only a comfortable home; and considering Mr. Collins's character, connections, and situation in life, I am convinced that my chance of happiness with him is as fair as most people can boast on entering the marriage state."
Charlotte Lucas, PP

In as short a time as Mr. Collins's long speeches would allow, every thing was settled between them to the satisfaction of both; and as they entered the house, he earnestly entreated her to Name the day that was to make him the happiest of men; and though such a solicitation must be waved for the present, the lady felt no inclination to trifle

with his happiness. The stupidity with which he was favoured by Nature must guard his courtship from any charm that could make a woman wish for its continuance; and Miss Lucas, who accepted him solely from the pure and disinterested desire of an establishment, cared not how soon that establishment were gained.
PP

Marriage plotting

The Lady Susan I congratulate you on Mr. De Courcy's arrival, & I advise you by all means to marry him; his Father's Estate is, we know, considerable, & I believe certainly entailed. Sir Reginald is very infirm, & not likely to stand in your way long. I hear the young Man well spoken of; & tho' no one can really deserve you, my dearest Susan, Mr. De Courcy may be worth having.
LS

"A very little trouble on your side secures him. Perhaps just at present he may be undecided; the smallness of your fortune may make him hang back; his friends may all advise him against it. But some of those little attentions and encouragements which ladies can so easily give will fix him, in spite of himself. And there can be no reason why you should not try for him. . . . It is a match that must give universal satisfaction. In short, it is a kind of thing that"—lowering his voice to an important whisper—"will be exceedingly welcome to ALL PARTIES."
John Dashwood, SS

Marriage potential

"Catherine would make a sad, heedless young housekeeper

to be sure," was her mother's foreboding remark; but quick was the consolation of there being nothing like practice.
Mrs. Morland, NA

Marriage proposals

"I am not now to learn," replied Mr. Collins, with a formal wave of the hand, "that it is usual with young ladies to reject the addresses of the man whom they secretly mean to accept, when he first applies for their favour; and that sometimes the refusal is repeated a second or even a third time. I am therefore by no means discouraged by what you have just said, and shall hope to lead you to the altar ere long.
Mr. Collins, PP

"A woman is not to marry a man merely because she is asked, or because he is attached to her, and can write a tolerable letter."
Emma Woodhouse, EM

"I lay it down as a general rule, Harriet, that if a woman doubts as to whether she should accept a man or not, she certainly ought to refuse him. If she can hesitate as to 'Yes,' she ought to say 'No' directly."
Emma Woodhouse, EM

"Oh! to be sure," cried Emma, "it is always incomprehensible to a man that a woman should ever refuse an offer of marriage. A man always imagines a woman to be ready for any body who asks her."
Emma Woodhouse, EM

Second marriage

He had never been an unhappy man; his own temper had secured him from that, even in his first marriage; but his second must shew him how delightful a well-judging and truly amiable woman could be, and must give him the pleasantest proof of its being a great deal better to choose than to be chosen, to excite gratitude than to feel it.
EM

Matchmaking

"Invite him to dinner, Emma, and help him to the best of the fish and the chicken, but leave him to chuse his own wife. Depend upon it, a man of six or seven-and-twenty can take care of himself."
George Knightley, EM

It would be an excellent match, for HE was rich, and SHE was handsome. Mrs. Jennings had been anxious to see Colonel Brandon well married, ever since her connection with Sir John first brought him to her knowledge; and she was always anxious to get a good husband for every pretty girl.
SS

Mr. Knightley shook his head at her. Her father fondly replied, "Ah! my dear, I wish you would not make matches and foretell things, for whatever you say always comes to pass. Pray do not make any more matches."
Mr. Woodhouse, EM

The first error and the worst lay at her door. It was foolish, it was wrong, to take so active a part in bringing any two people together. It was adventuring too far, assuming too

much, making light of what ought to be serious, a trick of what ought to be simple.
EM

"And you have forgotten one matter of joy to me," said Emma, "and a very considerable one—that I made the match myself. I made the match, you know, four years ago; and to have it take place, and be proved in the right, when so many people said Mr. Weston would never marry again, may comfort me for any thing."
Emma Woodhouse, EM

Mrs. Jennings was a widow with an ample jointure. She had only two daughters, both of whom she had lived to see respectably married, and she had now therefore nothing to do but to marry all the rest of the world. In the promotion of this object she was zealously active, as far as her ability reached; and missed no opportunity of projecting weddings among all the young people of her acquaintance. She was remarkably quick in the discovery of attachments, and had enjoyed the advantage of raising the blushes and the vanity of many a young lady by insinuations of her power over such a young man . . .
SS

Matrimony and Celibacy

In a review of the two houses, as they appeared to her before the end of a week, Fanny was tempted to apply to them Dr. Johnson's celebrated judgment as to matrimony and celibacy, and say, that though Mansfield Park might have some pains, Portsmouth could have no pleasures.
MP

Maturity

Anne hoped she had outlived the age of blushing; but the age of emotion she certainly had not.
PER

Medicine

Mrs. Jennings, though regretting that she had not been five minutes earlier, was satisfied with the compromise; and Elinor, as she swallowed the chief of it, reflected, that though its effects on a colicky gout were, at present, of little importance to her, its healing powers, on a disappointed heart might be as reasonably tried on herself as on her sister.
SS

Melancholy

Such violence of affliction indeed could not be supported for ever; it sunk within a few days into a calmer melancholy; but these employments, to which she daily recurred, her solitary walks and silent meditations, still produced occasional effusions of sorrow as lively as ever.
SS

Memory

"Perhaps I did not always love him so well as I do now. But in such cases as these, a good memory is unpardonable."
Elizabeth Bennet, PP

Men

He seems a very harmless sort of young man, nothing to
like or dislike in him—goes out shooting or hunting with
the two others all the morning, and plays at whist and makes
queer faces in the evening.
JAL

She was persuaded that any tolerably pleasing young woman
who had listened and seemed to feel for him would have
received the same compliment. He had an affectionate
heart. He must love somebody.
PER

"Men have had every advantage of us in telling their own
story. Education has been theirs in so much higher a degree;
the pen has been in their hands."
Anne Elliot, PER

Men and aging

"But then, is not it the same with many other professions,
perhaps most other? Soldiers, in active service, are not at all
better off: and even in the quieter professions, there is a toil
and a labour of the mind, if not of the body, which seldom
leaves a man's looks to the Natural effect of time."
Mrs. Clay, PER

Men and asking directions

"Bertram," said Crawford . . . "I have never told you what
happened to me yesterday in my ride home . . . I told you I
lost my way after passing that old farmhouse with the yew-

trees, because I can never bear to ask; but I have not told you that, with my usual luck—for I never do wrong without gaining by it—I found myself in due time in the very place which I had a curiosity to see. . . . I found myself, in short, in Thornton Lacey."

"It sounds like it," said Edmund; "but which way did you turn after passing Sewell's farm?"

"I answer no such irrelevant and insidious questions; though were I to answer all that you could put in the course of an hour, you would never be able to prove that it was not Thornton Lacey—for such it certainly was."

"You inquired, then?"

"No, I never inquire. But I told a man mending a hedge that it was Thornton Lacey, and he agreed to it."

Henry Crawford, Edmund Bertram, MP

Men and character

"So unlike what a man should be!—None of that upright integrity, that strict adherence to truth and principle, that disdain of trick and littleness, which a man should display in every transaction of his life."

Emma Woodhouse, EM

Men and dining

Most strange indeed!—But there is, I believe, in many men, especially single men, such an inclination—such a passion for dining out—a dinner engagement is so high in the class of their pleasures, their employments, their dignities, almost their duties, that any thing gives way to it."

Emma Woodhouse, EM

Men and fortune

But there certainly are not so many men of large fortune in the world as there are pretty women to deserve them.
MP

Men and manners

For the rest of his character and habits, they were marked, as far as Elinor could perceive, with no traits at all unusual in his sex and time of life. He was nice in his eating, uncertain in his hours; fond of his child, though affecting to slight it; and idled away the mornings at billiards, which ought to have been devoted to business. She liked him, however, upon the whole, much better than she had expected, and in her heart was not sorry that she could like him no more;— not sorry to be driven by the observation of his Epicurism, his selfishness, and his conceit.
SS

Men and nature

"What are men to rocks and mountains?"
Elizabeth Bennet, PP

Men and women

Maria, with only Mr. Rushworth to attend to her, [was] doomed to the repeated details of his day's sport, good or bad, his boast of his dogs, his jealousy of his neighbours, his doubts of their [hunting] qualifications, and his zeal after poachers—subjects which will not find their way to female

feelings without some talent on one side, or some attachment on the other.
MP

The ladies here probably exchanged looks which meant, "Men never know when things are dirty or not;" and the gentlemen perhaps thought each to himself, "Women will have their little nonsenses and needless cares."
EM

The Mr. Musgroves had their game to guard, and to destroy, their horses, dogs, and newspapers to engage them; and the females were fully occupied in all the other common subjects of housekeeping, neighbours, dress, dancing, and music.
PER

There were Mr. and Mrs. Weston; delighted to see her and receive her approbation, very busy and very happy in their different way; she, in some little distress; and he, finding every thing perfect.
EM

"You could not make *me* happy, and I am convinced that I am the last woman in the world who would make *you* so."
Elizabeth Bennet, PP

"No, no, it is not man's Nature. I will not allow it to be more man's Nature than woman's to be inconstant and forget those they do love, or have loved. I believe the reverse. I believe in a true analogy between our bodily frames and our mental; and that as our bodies are the strongest, so are our feelings; capable of bearing most rough usage, and riding out the heaviest weather."

"Your feelings may be the strongest," replied Anne, "but the same spirit of analogy will authorise me to assert that

ours are the most tender. Man is more robust than woman, but he is not longer lived; which exactly explains my view of the Nature of their attachments. Nay, it would be too hard upon you, if it were otherwise. You have difficulties, and privations, and dangers enough to struggle with. You are always labouring and toiling, exposed to every risk and hardship. Your home, country, friends, all quitted. Neither time, nor health, nor life, to be called your own. It would be hard, indeed . . . if woman's feelings were to be added to all this."
Captain Harville, Anne Elliot, PER

"Eliza Bennet," said Miss Bingley, when the door was closed on her,"is one of those young ladies who seek to recommend themselves to the other sex by undervaluing their own, and with many men, I dare say, it succeeds. But, in my opinion, it is a paltry device, a very mean art."

"Undoubtedly," replied Darcy, to whom this remark was chiefly addressed, "there is meanness in *all* the arts which ladies sometimes condescend to employ for captivation. Whatever bears affinity to cunning is despicable."
Caroline Bingley, Fitzwilliam Darcy, PP

"I am sick of them all. Thank Heaven! I am going tomorrow where I shall find a man who has not one agreeable quality, who has neither manner nor sense to recommend him. Stupid men are the only ones worth knowing, after all."
Elizabeth Bennet, PP

"Let him have all the perfections in the world, I think it ought not to be set down as certain that a man must be acceptable to every woman he may happen to like himself."
Fanny Price, MP

There was one gentleman, an officer of the Cheshire, a very good-looking young man, who, I was told, wanted very much to be introduced to me, but as he did not want it quite enough to take much trouble in effecting it, we never could bring it about.

JAL

But Catherine did not know her own advantages—did not know that a good-looking girl, with an affectionate heart and a very ignorant mind, cannot fail of attracting a clever young man, unless circumstances are particularly untoward.

NA

Men's vanity

Thorpe's ideas then all reverted to the merits of his own equipage, and she was called on to admire the spirit and freedom with which his horse moved along, and the ease which his paces, as well as the excellence of the springs, gave the motion of the carriage. She followed him in all his admiration as well as she could. To go before or beyond him was impossible. His knowledge and her ignorance of the subject, his rapidity of expression, and her diffidence of herself put that out of her power; she could strike out nothing new in commendation, but she readily echoed whatever he chose to assert, and it was finally settled between them without any difficulty that his equipage was altogether the most complete of its kind in England, his carriage the neatest, his horse the best goer, and himself the best coachman.

NA

Misanthropy

"The more I see of the world, the more am I dissatisfied with it; and every day confirms my belief of the inconsis-

tency of all human characters, and of the little dependence
that can be placed on the appearance of either merit or
sense."
Elizabeth Bennet, PP

I cannot anyhow continue to find people agreeable; I respect Mrs. Chamberlayne for doing her hair well, but cannot feel a more tender sentiment. Miss Langley is like any
other short girl, with a broad nose and wide mouth, fashionable dress and exposed bosom. Adm. Stanhope is a gentle-
man-like man, but then his legs are too short and his tail too
long.
JAL

Misconduct and Wanting to Explain

Feelings rather Natural than heroic possessed her; instead
of considering her own dignity injured by this ready condemnation—instead of proudly resolving, in conscious innocence, to show her resentment towards him who could
harbour a doubt of it, to leave to him all the trouble of seek-
ing an explanation, and to enlighten him on the past only
by avoiding his sight, or flirting with somebody else—she
took to herself all the shame of misconduct, or at least of its
appearance, and was only eager for an opportunity of explaining its cause.
NA

Miserliness

He so frequently talked of the increasing expenses of housekeeping, and of the perpetual demands upon his purse,
which a man of any consequence in the world was beyond

calculation exposed to, that he seemed rather to stand in need of more money himself than to have any design of giving money away.
SS

As far as walking, talking, and contriving reached, she was thoroughly benevolent, and nobody knew better how to dictate liberality to others; but her love of money was equal to her love of directing, and she knew quite as well how to save her own as to spend that of her friends.
MP

Misrepresentation

"I have not wanted syllables where actions have spoken so plainly. Has not his behaviour to Marianne and to all of us, for at least the last fortnight, declared that he loved and considered her as his future wife, and that he felt for us the attachment of the nearest relation? Have we not perfectly understood each other? Has not my consent been daily asked by his looks, his manner, his attentive and affectionate respect? My Elinor, is it possible to doubt their engagement? How could such a thought occur to you? How is it to be supposed that Willoughby, persuaded as he must be of your sister's love, should leave her, and leave her perhaps for months, without telling her of his affection;—that they should part without a mutual exchange of confidence?"
Mrs. Dashwood, SS

Mistresses

She found his manners very pleasing indeed.—The little flaw of having a Mistress now living with him at Ashdown

Park, seems to be the only unpleasing circumstance about him.
JAL

Money and Happiness

"Strange that it would!" cried Marianne. "What have wealth or grandeur to do with happiness?"

"Grandeur has but little," said Elinor, "but wealth has much to do with it."

"Elinor, for shame!" said Marianne, "money can only give happiness where there is nothing else to give it. Beyond a competence, it can afford no real satisfaction, as far as mere self is concerned."
Marianne Dashwood, Elinor Dashwood, SS

Morals

"We do not look in great cities for our best morality."
Edmund Bertram, MP

Mothers

"My mother's deafness is very trifling you see—just nothing at all. By only raising my voice, and saying any thing two or three times over, she is sure to hear; but then she is used to my voice. But it is very remarkable that she should always hear Jane better than she does me."
Miss Bates, EM

"Your mother will secure to you, in time, that independence you are so anxious for; it is her duty, and it will, it must ere

long become her happiness to prevent your whole youth from being wasted in discontent. How much may not a few months do?"
Mrs. Dashwood, SS

After a proper resistance on the part of Mrs. Ferrars, just so violent and so steady as to preserve her from that reproach which she always seemed fearful of incurring, the reproach of being too amiable, Edward was admitted to her presence, and pronounced to be again her son.
SS

Motherly pride

Fortunately for those who pay their court through such foibles, a fond mother, though, in pursuit of praise for her children, the most rapacious of human beings, is likewise the most credulous; her demands are exorbitant; but she will swallow any thing; and the excessive affection and endurance of the Miss Steeles towards her offspring were viewed therefore by Lady Middleton without the smallest surprise or distrust. She saw with maternal complacency all the impertinent encroachments and mischievous tricks to which her cousins submitted. She saw their sashes untied, their hair pulled about their ears, their work-bags searched, and their knives and scissors stolen away, and felt no doubt of its being a reciprocal enjoyment.
SS

Mothers and Daughters

It was contrary to every doctrine of her's that difference of fortune should keep any couple asunder who were at-

tracted by resemblance of disposition; and that Elinor's merit should not be acknowledged by every one who knew her, was to her comprehension impossible.
SS

In vain did Elizabeth endeavour to check the rapidity of her mother's words, or persuade her to describe her felicity in a less audible whisper; for to her inexpressible vexation, she could perceive that the chief of it was overheard by Mr. Darcy, who sat opposite to them. . . . Nothing that she could say, however, had any influence. Her mother would talk of her views in the same intelligible tone. Elizabeth blushed and blushed again with shame and vexation.
PP

Some mothers might have encouraged the intimacy from motives of interest, for Edward Ferrars was the eldest son of a man who had died very rich; and some might have re-pressed it from motives of prudence, for, except a trifling sum, the whole of his fortune depended on the will of his mother. But Mrs. Dashwood was alike uninfluenced by ei-ther consideration. It was enough for her that he appeared to be amiable, that he loved her daughter, and that Elinor returned the partiality.
SS

"Why do you not ask Marianne at once," said she, "whether she is or she is not engaged to Willoughby? From you, her mother, and so kind, so indulgent a mother, the question could not give offence. It would be the Natural result of your affection for her. She used to be all unreserve, and to you more especially."
Elinor Dashwood, SS

Nothing could console and nothing appease her.—Nor did that day wear out her resentment. A week elapsed before she could see Elizabeth without scolding her, a month passed

away before she could speak to Sir William or Lady Lucas
without being rude, and many months were gone before
she could at all forgive their daughter.
PP

When the hour of departure drew near, the maternal anxiety of Mrs. Morland will be Naturally supposed to be most
severe. A thousand alarming presentiments of evil to her
beloved Catherine from this terrific separation must op-
press her heart with sadness, and drown her in tears for the
last day or two of their being together; and advice of the
most important and applicable Nature must of course flow
from her wise lips in their parting conference in her closet.
Cautions against the violence of such noblemen and baronets as delight in forcing young ladies away to some re-
mote farm-house, must, at such a moment, relieve the
fulness of her heart. Who would not think so? But Mrs.
Morland knew so little of lords and baronets, that she entertained no notion of their general mischievousness, and was
wholly unsuspicious of danger to her daughter from their
machinations. Her cautions were confined to the following
points. "I beg, Catherine, you will always wrap yourself up
very warm about the throat, when you come from the
rooms at night; and I wish you would try to keep some account of the money you spend; I will give you this little
book on purpose."
Mrs. Morland, NA

Mothers-in-law

Elinor's curiosity to see Mrs. Ferrars was satisfied . . . She
had seen enough of her pride, her meanness, and her determined prejudice against herself, to comprehend all the difficulties that must have perplexed the engagement, and

retarded the marriage, of Edward and herself, had he been otherwise free;—and she had seen almost enough to be thankful for her OWN sake, that one greater obstacle preserved her from suffering under any other of Mrs. Ferrars's creation, preserved her from all dependence upon her caprice, or any solicitude for her good opinion.
SS

Elinor placed all that was astonishing in this way of acting to his mother's account; and it was happy for her that he had a mother whose character was so imperfectly known to her, as to be the general excuse for every thing strange on the part of her son. . . . The shortness of his visit, the steadiness of his purpose in leaving them, originated in the same fettered inclination, the same inevitable necessity of temporizing with his mother. The old well-established grievance of duty against will, parent against child, was the cause of all. She would have been glad to know when these difficulties were to cease, this opposition was to yield,—when Mrs. Ferrars would be reformed, and her son be at liberty to be happy.
SS

Motivation

Henry smiled, and said, "How very little trouble it can give you to understand the motive of other people's actions."

"Why? What do you mean?"

"With you, it is not, How is such a one likely to be influenced, What is the inducement most likely to act upon such a person's feelings, age, situation, and probable habits of life considered—but, How should *I* be influenced, What would be my inducement in acting so and so?"
Henry Tilney, Catherine Morland, NA

Music

"I could not excuse a man's having more music than love—more ear than eye—a more acute sensibility to fine sounds than to my feelings."
Emma Woodhouse, EM

The events of this evening were not very remarkable. The party, like other musical parties, comprehended a great many people who had real taste for the performance, and a great many more who had none at all; and the performers themselves were, as usual, in their own estimation, and that of their immediate friends, the first private performers in England.
SS

To the Great House accordingly they went, to sit the full half hour in the old-fashioned square parlour, with a small carpet and shining floor, to which the present daughters of the house were gradually giving the proper air of confusion by a grand piano-forte and a harp, flower-stands and little tables placed in every direction. Oh! could the originals of the portraits against the wainscot, could the gentlemen in brown velvet and the ladies in blue satin have seen what was going on, have been conscious of such an overthrow of all order and neatness! The portraits themselves seemed to be staring in astonishment.
PER

Mutual Admiration

You are very good in wishing to see me at Ibthorp so soon, and I am equally good in wishing to come to you. I believe our merit in that respect is much upon a par, our self-denial mutually strong.
JAL

Nature

The trees, though not fully clothed, were in that delightful state, when further beauty is known to be at hand, and when, while much is actually given to the sight, more yet remains for the imagination.
MP

"To sit in the shade on a fine day and look upon verdure is the most perfect refreshment."
Fanny Price, MP

"The evergreen! How beautiful, how welcome, how wonderful the evergreen! When one thinks of it, how astonishing a variety of Nature! In some countries we know the tree that sheds its leaf is the variety, but that does not make it less amazing that the same soil and the same sun should nurture plants differing in the first rule and law of their existence. You will think me rhapsodising; but when I am out of doors, especially when I am sitting out of doors, I am very apt to get into this sort of wondering strain. One cannot fix one's eyes on the commonest Natural production without finding food for a rambling fancy."
Fanny Price, MP

Fanny agreed to it, and had the pleasure of seeing him continue at the window with her, in spite of the expected glee; and of having his eyes soon turned, like hers, towards the scene without, where all that was solemn, and soothing, and lovely, appeared in the brilliancy of an unclouded night, and the contrast of the deep shade of the woods. Fanny spoke her feelings. "Here's harmony!" said she; "here's repose! Here's what may leave all painting and all music behind, and what poetry only can attempt to describe! Here's what may tranquillise every care, and lift the heart to rapture! When I look out on such a night as this, I feel as if there

could be neither wickedness nor sorrow in the world; and there certainly would be less of both if the sublimity of Nature were more attended to, and people were carried more out of themselves by contemplating such a scene."
Fanny Price, MP

Neighbours

The Webbs are really gone! When I saw the waggons at the door, and thought of all the trouble they must have in moving, I began to reproach myself for not having liked them better; but since the waggons have disappeared my conscience has been closed again, and I am excessively glad they are gone.
JAL

Nervousness

"You mistake me, my dear. I have a high respect for your nerves. They are my old friends. I have heard you mention them with consideration these twenty years at least."
Mr. Bennet, PP

Noise

Everybody has their taste in noises as well as in other matters; and sounds are quite innoxious, or most distressing, by their sort rather than their quantity. When Lady Russell not long afterwards, was entering Bath on a wet afternoon, and driving through the long course of streets from the Old Bridge to Camden Place, amidst the dash of other carriages, the heavy rumble of carts and drays, the bawling of newspapermen, muffin-men and milkmen, and the ceaseless

clink of pattens, she made no complaint. No, these were noises which belonged to the winter pleasures; her spirits rose under their influence; and like Mrs. Musgrove, she was feeling, though not saying, that after being long in the country, nothing could be so good for her as a little quiet cheerfulness.
PER

The living in incessant noise was . . . the greatest misery of all. . . . Here everybody was noisy, every voice was loud excepting, perhaps, her mother's, which resembled the soft monotony of Lady Bertram's, only worn into fretfulness. Whatever was wanted was halloo'd for, and the servants halloo'd out their excuses from the kitchen. The doors were in constant banging, the stairs were never at rest, nothing was done without a clatter, nobody sat still, and nobody could command attention when they spoke.
MP

Novels

"Oh! It is only a novel! . . . only Cecilia, or Camilla, or Belinda"; or, in short, only some work in which . . . the most thorough knowledge of human Nature, the happiest delineation of its varieties, the liveliest effusions of wit and humour are conveyed to the world in the best chosen language.
NA

"The person, be it gentleman or lady, who has not pleasure in a good novel, must be intolerably stupid."
Henry Tilney, NA

As an inducement to subscribe, Mrs. Martin [the circulating-library proprietor] tells me that her collection is not to consist only of novels, but of every kind of literature, &c.;

She might have spared this pretension to our family, who are great novel-readers and not ashamed of being so; but it was necessary, I suppose, to the self-consequence of half her subscribers.
JAL

Novelists

And if a rainy morning deprived them of other enjoyments, they were still resolute in meeting in defiance of wet and dirt, and shut themselves up, to read novels together. Yes, novels; for I will not adopt that ungenerous and impolitic custom so common with novel-writers, of degrading by their contemptuous censure the very performances, to the number of which they are themselves adding—joining with their greatest enemies in bestowing the harshest epithets on such works, and scarcely ever permitting them to be read by their own heroine, who, if she accidentally take up a novel, is sure to turn over its insipid pages with disgust. Alas! If the heroine of one novel be not patronized by the heroine of another, from whom can she expect protection and regard? I cannot approve of it. Let us leave it to the reviewers to abuse such effusions of fancy at their leisure, and over every new novel to talk in threadbare strains of the trash with which the press now groans. Let us not desert one another; we are an injured body.
NA

Obesity

Personal size and mental sorrow have certainly no necessary proportions. A large bulky figure has as good a right to be in deep affliction, as the most graceful set of limbs in the world. But, fair or not fair, there are unbecoming conjunc-

tions, which reason will patronize in vain—which taste cannot tolerate—which ridicule will seize.
PER

Obligation

"He has those to please who must be pleased, and who between ourselves are sometimes to be pleased only by a good many sacrifices."
Mr. Weston, EM

Old Friends

The visit was paid, their acquaintance re-established, their interest in each other more than re-kindled. The first ten minutes had its awkwardness and its emotion. Twelve years were gone since they had parted, and each presented a somewhat different person from what the other had imagined. Twelve years had changed Anne from the blooming, silent, unformed girl of fifteen, to the elegant little woman of seven-and-twenty, with every beauty except bloom, and with manners as consciously right as they were invariably gentle; and twelve years had transformed the fine-looking, well-grown Miss Hamilton, in all the glow of health and confidence of superiority, into a poor, infirm, helpless widow, receiving the visit of her former protégée as a favour; but all that was uncomfortable in the meeting had soon passed away, and left only the interesting charm of remembering former partialities and talking over old times.
PER

Old Maids

"If I thought I should ever be like Miss Bates! so silly—so satisfied—so smiling—so prosing—so undistinguishing and unfastidious—and so apt to tell every thing relative to every body about me, I would marry to-morrow."
Emma Woodhouse, EM

"Never mind, Harriet, I shall not be a poor old maid; and it is poverty only which makes celibacy contemptible to a generous public! A single woman, with a very narrow income, must be a ridiculous, disagreeable old maid! the proper sport of boys and girls, but a single woman, of good fortune, is always respectable, and may be as sensible and pleasant as any body else."
Emma Woodhouse, EM

Opinion

"Where an opinion is general, it is usually correct."
Mary Crawford, MP

Optimism

"If things are going untowardly one month, they are sure to mend the next."
Mr. Weston, EM

Parents

"Come here, child," cried her father as she appeared. "I have sent for you on an affair of importance. I understand that Mr. Collins has made you an offer of marriage. Is it true?" Elizabeth replied that it was. "Very well—and this offer of marriage you have refused?"

"I have, Sir."

"Very well. We now come to the point. Your mother insists upon your accepting it. Is not it so, Mrs. Bennet?"

"Yes, or I will never see her again."

"An unhappy alternative is before you, Elizabeth. From this day you must be a stranger to one of your parents.— Your mother will never see you again if you do *not* marry Mr. Collins, and I will never see you again if you *do*."

Mr. Bennet, Elizabeth Bennet, Mrs. Bennet, PP

He was not in spirits, however; he praised their house, admired its prospect, was attentive, and kind; but still he was not in spirits. The whole family perceived it, and Mrs. Dashwood, attributing it to some want of liberality in his mother, sat down to table indignant against all selfish parents.

SS

Parties

We are to have a tiny party here tonight; I hate tiny parties—they force one into constant exertion.

JAL

"And when you get there, you must tell him at what time you would have him come for you again; and you had better name an early hour. You will not like staying late. You will get very tired when tea is over."

"But you would not wish me to come away before I am tired, papa?"

"Oh! no, my love; but you will soon be tired. There will be a great many people talking at once. You will not like the noise."

"But, my dear sir," cried Mr. Weston, "if Emma comes away early, it will be breaking up the party."

"And no great harm if it does," said Mr. Woodhouse. "The sooner every party breaks up, the better."
Mr. Woodhouse, Emma Woodhouse, Mr. Weston, EM

Parties and gossip

"This is the luxury of a large party," said she:—"one can get near every body, and say every thing. My dear Emma, I am longing to talk to you. I have been making discoveries and forming plans, just like yourself, and I must tell them while the idea is fresh."
Mrs. Weston, EM

Parting

"Come, come; this is all an effusion of immediate want of spirits, Edward. You are in a melancholy humour, and fancy that any one unlike yourself must be happy. But remember that the pain of parting from friends will be felt by every body at times, whatever be their education or state.
Mrs. Dashwood, SS

Piety

"There is something in a chapel and chaplain so much in character with a great house, with one's ideas of what such a household should be! A whole family assembling regularly for the purpose of prayer is fine!"

"Very fine indeed," said Miss Crawford, laughing. "It must do the heads of the family a great deal of good to force all the poor housemaids and footmen to leave business and

pleasure, and say their prayers here twice a day, while they are inventing excuses themselves for staying away."
Fanny Price, Mary Crawford, MP

Piety and parsons

"Cannot you imagine with what unwilling feelings the former belles of the house of Rushworth did many a time repair to this chapel? The young Mrs. Eleanors and Mrs. Bridgets—starched up into seeming piety, but with heads full of something very different—especially if the poor chaplain were not worth looking at—and, in those days, I fancy parsons were very inferior even to what they are now."
Mary Crawford, MP

Pique

I shall not tell you anything more of Wm. Digweed's china, as your silence on the subject makes you unworthy of it.
JAL

Your silence on the subject of our ball makes me suppose your curiosity too great for words.
JAL

Plainness

He hoped she might make some amends for the many very plain faces he was continually passing in the streets. The worst of Bath was the number of its plain women. He did not mean to say that there were no pretty women, but the number of the plain was out of all proportion. He had frequently observed, as he walked, that one handsome face would be followed by thirty, or five-and-thirty frights; and once, as he had stood in a shop on Bond Street, he had

counted eighty-seven women go by, one after another, without there being a tolerable face among them. It had been a frosty morning, to be sure, a sharp frost, which hardly one woman in a thousand could stand the test of. But still, there certainly were a dreadful multitude of ugly women in Bath.
PER

Pleasure

"That is the case with us all, papa. One half of the world cannot understand the pleasures of the other."
Emma Woodhouse, EM

Pleasure and pain

"The last hours were certainly very painful," replied Anne; "but when pain is over, the remembrance of it often becomes a pleasure. One does not love a place the less for having suffered in it, unless it has been all suffering, nothing but suffering, which was by no means the case at Lyme. We were only in anxiety and distress during the last two hours, and previously there had been a great deal of enjoyment. So much novelty and beauty! I have travelled so little, that every fresh place would be interesting to me; but there is real beauty at Lyme; and in short . . . altogether my impressions of the place are very agreeable."
Anne Elliot, PER

Politics

Delighted with her progress, and fearful of wearying her with too much wisdom at once, Henry suffered the subject to decline, and by an easy transition from a piece of rocky

fragment and the withered oak which he had placed near its summit, to oaks in general, to forests, the enclosure of them, waste lands, crown lands and government, he shortly found himself arrived at politics; and from politics, it was an easy step to silence.
NA

Popularity

And he, the very handsomest man that ever was, and a man that every body looks up to, quite like Mr. Knightley! His company so sought after, that every body says he need not eat a single meal by himself if he does not chuse it; that he has more invitations than there are days in the week.
EM

Their acquaintance was exceedingly sought after. Everybody was wanting to visit them. They had drawn back from many introductions, and still were perpetually having cards left by people of whom they knew nothing.
PER

Post Office

"The post-office is a wonderful establishment! . . . The regularity and despatch of it! If one thinks of all that it has to do, and all that it does so well, it is really astonishing! . . . So seldom that any negligence or blunder appears! So seldom that a letter, among the thousands that are constantly passing about the kingdom, is even carried wrong—and not one in a million, I suppose, actually lost! And when one considers the variety of hands, and of bad hands too, that are to be deciphered, it increases the wonder."
Jane Fairfax, EM

Poverty

"And the distinction is not quite so much against the candour and common sense of the world as appears at first; for a very narrow income has a tendency to contract the mind, and sour the temper. Those who can barely live, and who live perforce in a very small, and generally very inferior, society, may well be illiberal and cross."
Emma Woodhouse, EM

I find, on looking into my affairs, that instead of being very rich I am likely to be very poor . . . as we are to meet in Canterbury I need not have mentioned this. It is as well, however, to prepare you for the sight of a sister sunk in poverty, that it may not overcome your spirits.
JAL

Pragmatism

Marianne Dashwood was born to an extraordinary fate. She was born to discover the falsehood of her own opinions, and to counteract, by her conduct, her most favourite maxims. She was born to overcome an affection formed so late in life as at seventeen, and with no sentiment superior to strong esteem and lively friendship, voluntarily to give her hand to another!
SS

Pride

"Pride," observed Mary, who piqued herself upon the solidity of her reflections, "is a very common failing I believe. By all that I have ever read, I am convinced that it is very common indeed, that human Nature is particularly prone to it,

and that there are very few of us who do not cherish a feeling of self-complacency on the score of some quality or other, real or imaginary."
Mary Bennet, PP

"And this," cried Darcy, as he walked with quick steps across the room, "is your opinion of me! This is the estimation in which you hold me! I thank you for explaining it so fully. My faults, according to this calculation, are heavy indeed! But perhaps," added he, stopping in his walk, and turning towards her, "these offences might have been overlooked, had not your pride been hurt by my honest confession of the scruples that had long prevented my forming any serious design. These bitter accusations might have been suppressed, had I with greater policy concealed my struggles, and flattered you into the belief of my being impelled by unqualified, unalloyed inclination—by reason, by reflection, by every thing."
—Fitzwilliam Darcy, PP

Prudence

"I am now convinced, my dear aunt, that I have never been much in love; for had I really experienced that pure and elevating passion, I should at present detest his very Name, and wish him all manner of evil. But my feelings are not only cordial towards *him*; they are even impartial towards Miss King. I cannot find out that I hate her at all, or that I am in the least unwilling to think her a very good sort of girl. There can be no love in all this."
Elizabeth Bennet, PP

"You are too sensible a girl, Lizzy, to fall in love merely because you are warned against it; and, therefore, I am not afraid of speaking openly."
Mrs. Gardiner, PP

Prudence and romance

She had been forced into prudence in her youth, she learned romance as she grew older—the Natural sequel of an un-Natural beginning.
PER

Qualities in a Man

"I could not be happy with a man whose taste did not in every point coincide with my own. He must enter into all my feelings; the same books, the same music must charm us both."
Marianne Dashwood, SS

Quarrels and Making Up

She hoped they might now become friends again. She thought it was time to make up. Making-up indeed would not do. She certainly had not been in the wrong, and he would never own that he had. Concession must be out of the question; but it was time to appear to forget that they had ever quarreled.
EM

Reason

"Every impulse of feeling should be guided by reason; and, in my opinion, exertion should always be in proportion to what is required."
Mary Bennet, PP

Recklessness

But Marianne abhorred all concealment where no real disgrace could attend unreserve; and to aim at the restraint of sentiments which were not in themselves illaudable, appeared to her not merely an unnecessary effort, but a disgraceful subjection of reason to common-place and mistaken notions. Willoughby thought the same; and their behaviour at all times, was an illustration of their opinions.
SS

Reflection

Reflection must be reserved for solitary hours; whenever she was alone, she gave way to it as the greatest relief; and not a day went by without a solitary walk, in which she might indulge in all the delight of unpleasant recollection.
PP

Reform

It was rather too late in the day to set about being simple-minded and ignorant; but she left her [Harriet] with every previous resolution confirmed of being humble and discreet, and repressing imagination all the rest of her life.
EM

She saw ... that there had been a period of his life (and probably not a short one) when he had been, at least, careless in all serious matters; and, though he might now think very differently, who could answer for the true sentiments of a clever, cautious man, grown old enough to appreciate a fair character? How could it ever be ascertained that his mind was truly cleansed?
PER

Regionalism

Anne had not wanted this visit to Uppercross, to learn that a removal from one set of people to another, though at a distance of only three miles, will often include a total change of conversation, opinion, and idea.
PER

Regret

My Understanding is at length restored, & teaches me no less to abhor the Artifices which had subdued me than to despise myself for the weakness on which their strength was founded.
LS

"Every line, every word was—in the hackneyed metaphor which their dear writer, were she here, would forbid—a dagger to my heart. To know that Marianne was in town was—in the same language—a thunderbolt.—Thunderbolts and daggers!—what a reproof would she have given me!—her taste, her opinions—I believe they are better known to me than my own,—and I am sure they are dearer."
John Willoughby, SS

"I considered the past: I saw in my own behaviour, since the beginning of our acquaintance with him last autumn, nothing but a series of imprudence towards myself, and want of kindness to others."
Marianne Dashwood, SS

Rejection

Catherine's swelling heart needed relief. In Eleanor's presence friendship and pride had equally restrained her tears,

but no sooner was she gone than they burst forth in torrents. Turned from the house, and in such a way! Without any reason that could justify, any apology that could atone for the abruptness, the rudeness, Nay, the insolence of it . . . What could all this mean but an intentional affront?
NA

"Which do you mean?" and turning round, he looked for a moment at Elizabeth, till catching her eye, he withdrew his own and coldly said, "She is tolerable; but not handsome enough to tempt *me*; and I am in no humour at present to give consequence to young ladies who are slighted by other men. You had better return to your partner and enjoy her smiles, for you are wasting your time with me."
Fitzwilliam Darcy, PP

Relationships

"That's easily said, and easily felt by you, who have always been your own master. You are the worst judge in the world, Mr. Knightley, of the difficulties of dependence. You do not know what it is to have tempers to manage."
Emma Woodhouse, EM

Relief

The tone, the look, with which "Thank God!" was uttered by Captain Wentworth, Anne was sure could never be forgotten by her; nor the sight of him afterwards, as he sat near a table, leaning over it with folded arms and face concealed, as if overpowered by the various feelings of his soul, and trying by prayer and reflection to calm them.
PER

Remarriage

"Your sister, I understand, does not approve of second attachments."

"No," replied Elinor, "her opinions are all romantic."

"Or rather, as I believe, she considers them impossible to exist."

"I believe she does. But how she contrives it without reflecting on the character of her own father, who had himself two wives, I know not."

Colonel Brandon, Elinor Dashwood, SS

Renovations

"The house must be turned to front the east instead of the north—the entrance and principal rooms, I mean, must be on that side, where the view is really very pretty; I am sure it may be done. And *there* must be your approach, through what is at present the garden. You must make a new garden at what is now the back of the house; which will be giving it the best aspect in the world, sloping to the Southeast. The ground seems precisely formed for it. I rode fifty yards up the lane, between the church and the house, in order to look about me; and saw how it might all be. Nothing can be easier. The meadows beyond what will be the garden, as well as what now is, sweeping round from the lane I stood in to the north-east, that is, to the principal road through the village, must be all laid together, of course; very pretty meadows they are, finely sprinkled with timber."

Henry Crawford, MP

Renting

The undesirableness of any other house in the same neighbourhood for Sir Walter was certainly much strengthened

by one part, and a very material part of the scheme, which had been happily engrafted on the beginning. He was not only to quit his home, but to see it in the hands of others; a trial of fortitude, which stronger heads than Sir Walter's have found too much. Kellynch Hall was to be let.
PER

Reputation

"We must persuade Henry to marry her . . . and when once married, and properly supported by her own family, she may recover her footing in society to a certain degree. In some circles, we know, she would never be admitted, but with good dinners, and large parties, there will always be those who will be glad of her acquaintance; and there is, undoubtedly, more liberality and candour on those points than formerly."
Edmund Bertram, quoting Mary Crawford, MP

Reserve

"It is a most repulsive quality, indeed," said he. "Oftentimes very convenient, no doubt, but never pleasing. There is safety in reserve, but no attraction. One cannot love a reserved person."
Frank Churchill, EM

Though perfectly well-bred, she was reserved, cold, and had nothing to say for herself beyond the most commonplace inquiry or remark.
SS

Anne did not wish for more of such looks and speeches. His cold politeness, his ceremonious grace, were worse than anything.
PER

Mr Elliot was rational, discreet, polished, but he was not open. There was never any burst of feeling, any warmth of indignation or delight, at the evil or good of others. This, to Anne, was a decided imperfection.
PER

She was, besides, which was the worst of all, so cold, so cautious! There was no getting at her real opinion. Wrapt up in a cloak of politeness, she seemed determined to hazard nothing. She was disgustingly, was suspiciously reserved.
EM

This had just taken place and with great cordiality, when John Knightley made his appearance, and "How d'ye do, George?" and "John, how are you?" succeeded in the true English style, burying under a calmness that seemed all but indifference, the real attachment which would have led either of them, if requisite, to do every thing for the good of the other.
EM

Sir Thomas did not know what was wanting, because, though a truly anxious father, he was not outwardly affectionate, and the reserve of his manner repressed all the flow of their spirits before him.
MP

Resignation

"Resignation to inevitable evils is the duty of us all."
Mr. Collins, PP

Resolve

Elinor honoured her for a plan which originated so nobly as this; though smiling to see the same eager fancy which had been leading her to the extreme of languid indolence and selfish repining, now at work in introducing excess into a scheme of such rational employment and virtuous self-control.

SS

Rivalry

Henry Crawford had trifled with her feelings; but she had very long allowed and even sought his attentions, with a jealousy of her sister so reasonable as ought to have been their cure; and now that the conviction of his preference for Maria had been forced on her, she submitted to it without any alarm for Maria's situation, or any endeavour at rational tranquillity for herself. She either sat in gloomy silence, wrapped in such gravity as nothing could subdue, no curiosity touch, no wit amuse.

MP

The sister with whom she was used to be on easy terms was now become her greatest enemy: they were alienated from each other; and Julia was not superior to the hope of some distressing end to the attentions which were still carrying on there, some punishment to Maria for conduct so shameful towards herself as well as towards Mr. Rushworth. With no material fault of temper, or difference of opinion, to prevent their being very good friends while their interests were the same, the sisters, under such a trial as this, had not affection or principle enough to make them merciful or just, to give them honour or compassion. Maria felt her triumph, and pursued her purpose, careless of Julia; and Julia could never see Maria distinguished by Henry Crawford without trusting that it would create jealousy, and bring a public disturbance at last.

MP

Romance

The anxieties of common life began soon to succeed to the alarms of romance.
NA

Carrying a torch

For Marianne, however—in spite of his incivility in surviving her loss—he always retained that decided regard which interested him in every thing that befell her, and made her his secret standard of perfection in woman;—and many a rising beauty would be slighted by him in after-days as bearing no comparison with Mrs. Brandon.
SS

Gratitude, not merely for having once loved her, but for loving her still well enough to forgive all the petulance and acrimony of her manner in rejecting him, and all the unjust accusations accompanying her rejection. . . . Such a change in a man of so much pride excited not only astonishment but gratitude—for to love, ardent love, it must be attributed; and as such, its impression on her was of a sort to be encouraged, as by no means unpleasing, though it could not be exactly defined. She respected, she esteemed, she was grateful to him; she felt a real interest in his welfare; and she only wanted to know how far she wished that welfare to depend upon herself, and how far it would be for the happiness of both that she should employ the power, which her fancy told her she still possessed, of bringing on the renewal of his addresses.
PP

Romance and making do

Had she intended ever to marry him, it might have been worth while to pause and consider, and try to understand the value of his preference, and the character of his temper; but for all the purposes of their acquaintance, he was quite amiable enough.
EM

Romance novels

She saw that the infatuation had been created, the mischief settled, long before her quitting Bath, and it seemed as if the whole might be traced to the influence of that sort of reading which she had there indulged.
NA

Romantic Disbelief

As for Lucy Steele, she considered her so totally unamiable, so absolutely incapable of attaching a sensible man, that she could not be persuaded at first to believe, and afterwards to pardon, any former affection of Edward for her. She would not even admit it to have been Natural; and Elinor left her to be convinced that it was so, by that which only could convince her, a better knowledge of mankind.
SS

Room of One's Own

The comfort of it in her hours of leisure was extreme. She could go there after anything unpleasant below, and find immediate consolation in some pursuit, or some train of

thought at hand. Her plants, her books—of which she had been a collector from the first hour of her commanding a shilling—her writing-desk, and her works of charity and ingenuity, were all within her reach; or if indisposed for employment, if nothing but musing would do, she could scarcely see an object in that room which had not an interesting remembrance connected with it. Everything was a friend, or bore her thoughts to a friend . . .
MP

Sailors

She gloried in being a sailor's wife, but she must pay the tax of quick alarm for belonging to that profession which is, if possible, more distinguished in its domestic virtues than in its National importance.
PER

"The sea is no beautifier, certainly; sailors do grow old betimes; I have observed it; they soon lose the look of youth."
Mrs. Clay, PER

"The Navy, I think, who have done so much for us, have at least an equal claim with any other set of men, for all the comforts and all the privileges which any home can give. Sailors work hard enough for their comforts, we must all allow."
Anne Elliot, PER

"Yes; it is in two points offensive to me; I have two strong grounds of objection to it. First, as being the means of bringing persons of obscure birth into undue distinction, and raising men to honours which their fathers and grandfathers never dreamt of; and secondly, as it cuts up a man's youth and vigour most horribly; a sailor grows old sooner

than any other man. I have observed it all my life. A man is in greater danger in the Navy of being insulted by the rise of one whose father, his father might have disdained to speak to, and of becoming prematurely an object of disgust himself, than in any other line."
Sir Walter Elliot, PER

Scenery and Sentiment

A young woman, pretty, lively, with a harp as elegant as herself; and both placed near a window, cut down to the ground, and opening on a little lawn, surrounded in the rich foliage of summer, was enough to catch any man's heart. The season, the scene, the air, were all favourable to tenderness and sentiment.
MP

Sea

The party from Uppercross passing down by the now de-serted and melancholy looking rooms, and still descending, soon found themselves on the sea-shore; and lingering only, as all must linger and gaze on a first return to the sea, who ever deserved to look on it at all, proceeded towards the Cobb.
PER

Secrets

"There are secrets in all families."
Mr. Weston, EM

The necessity of concealing from her mother and Marianne, what had been entrusted in confidence to herself, though it obliged her to unceasing exertion, was no aggravation of Elinor's distress. On the contrary it was a relief to her, to be spared the communication of what would give such affliction to them, and to be saved likewise from hearing that condemnation of Edward, which would probably flow from the excess of their partial affection for herself, and which was more than she felt equal to support.

SS

"It is to be a secret, I conclude," said he. "These matters are always a secret, till it is found out that every body knows them."

Mr. Weston, EM

Security

I am glad you recollected to mention your being come home. My heart began to sink within me when I had got so far through your letter without its being mentioned. I was dreadfully afraid that you might be detained at Winchester by severe illness, confined to your bed perhaps, and quite unable to hold a pen, and only dating from Steventon in order, with a mistaken sort of tenderness, to deceive me. But now I have no doubt of your being at home.

JAL

Self-control

She could not be complying, she dreaded being quarrelsome; her heroism reached only to silence. She allowed him to talk, and arranged the glasses, and wrapped herself up, without opening her lips.

EM

Self-esteem

"Oh! I always deserve the best treatment, because I never put up with any other."
Emma Woodhouse, EM

Self-importance

When the ladies returned to the drawing room, there was little to be done but to hear Lady Catherine talk, which she did without any intermission till coffee came in, delivering her opinion on every subject in so decisive a manner as proved that she was not used to have her judgment controverted.
PP

Self-indulgence

How quick come the reasons for approving what we like!
PER

She was a woman who spent her days in sitting, nicely dressed, on a sofa, doing some long piece of needlework, of little use and no beauty, thinking more of her pug than her children, but very indulgent to the latter when it did not put herself to inconvenience, guided in everything important by Sir Thomas, and in smaller concerns by her sister. Had she possessed greater leisure for the service of her girls, she would probably have supposed it unnecessary, for they were under the care of a governess, with proper masters, and could want nothing more.
MP

Selfishness

"Selfishness must always be forgiven, you know, because there is no hope of a cure."
Mary Crawford, MP

The whole of Lucy's behaviour in the affair, and the prosperity which crowned it, therefore, may be held forth as a most encouraging instance of what an earnest, an unceasing attention to self-interest, however its progress may be apparently obstructed, will do in securing every advantage of fortune, with no other sacrifice than that of time and conscience.
SS

Self-pity

Everybody around her was gay and busy, prosperous and important; each had their object of interest, their part, their dress, their favourite scene, their friends and confederates: all were finding employment in consultations and comparisons, or diversion in the playful conceits they suggested. She alone was sad and insignificant: she had no share in anything; she might go or stay; she might be in the midst of their noise, or retreat from it to the solitude of the East room, without being seen or missed. She could almost think anything would have been preferable to this.
MP

Selling Books

Since I wrote last, my 2nd edition [of SS] has stared me in the face. I cannot help hoping that many will feel them-

selves obliged to buy it. I shall not mind imagining it a disagreeable duty to them, so as they do it.
JAL

Sense

Elinor, this eldest daughter, whose advice was so effectual, possessed a strength of understanding, and coolness of judgment, which qualified her, though only nineteen, to be the counsellor of her mother, and enabled her frequently to counteract, to the advantage of them all, that eagerness of mind in Mrs. Dashwood which must generally have led to imprudence. She had an excellent heart;—her disposition was affectionate, and her feelings were strong; but she knew how to govern them: it was a knowledge which her mother had yet to learn; and which one of her sisters had resolved never to be taught.
SS

Sensibility

Marianne's abilities were, in many respects, quite equal to Elinor's. She was sensible and clever; but eager in everything: her sorrows, her joys, could have no moderation. She was generous, amiable, interesting: she was everything but prudent.
SS

Sensitivity

Her feelings were very acute, and too little understood to be properly attended to. Nobody meant to be unkind, but nobody put themselves out of their way to secure her comfort.
MP

Separation

He knows nothing of his own destination, he says, but desires me to write directly, as the "Endymion" will probably sail in three or four days. He will receive my yesterday's letter, and I shall write again by this post to thank and reproach him. We shall be unbearably fine.
JAL

Servants

My mother looks forward with as much certainty as you can do to our keeping two maids ... We plan having a steady cook and a young, giddy housemaid, with a sedate, middle-aged man, who is to undertake the double office of husband to the former and sweetheart to the latter. No children, of course, to be allowed on either side.
JAL

Shame

Had she known nothing of Darcy, she could have borne the dread of Lydia's infamy somewhat better. It would have spared her, she thought, one sleepless night out of two.
PP

Short Skirts

You will find Captain ——————— a very respectable, well-meaning man, without much manner, his wife and sister all good humour and obligingness, and I hope since the fashion allows it with rather longer petticoats than last year.
JAL

Shyness

"Shyness is only the effect of a sense of inferiority in some way or other. If I could persuade myself that my manners were perfectly easy and graceful, I should not be shy."
Edward Ferrars, SS

Singularity

"What will he be doing, in fact, but what very many of our first families have done, or ought to do? There will be nothing singular in his case; and it is singularity which often makes the worst part of our suffering, as it always does of our conduct."
Lady Russell, PER

Sisters

How was Anne to set all these matters to rights? She could do little more than listen patiently, soften every grievance, and excuse each to the other; give them all hints of the forbearance necessary between such near neighbours, and make those hints broadest which were meant for her sister's benefit.
PER

On this subject I will only say further that my dearest sister, my tender, watchful, indefatigable nurse, has not been made ill by her exertions. As to what I owe her, and to the anxious affection of all my beloved family on this occasion, I can only cry over it, and pray to God to bless them more and more.
JAL

All this became gradually evident, and gradually placed Susan before her sister as an object of mingled compassion

and respect. That her manner was wrong, however, at times very wrong, her measures often ill-chosen and ill-timed, and her looks and language very often indefensible, Fanny could not cease to feel; but she began to hope they might be rectified.
MP

Sister's criticism

"Perhaps," said Marianne, "I may consider it with some surprise. Edward is very amiable, and I love him tenderly. But yet—he is not the kind of young man—there is something wanting—his figure is not striking; it has none of that grace which I should expect in the man who could seriously attach my sister. His eyes want all that spirit, that fire, which at once announce virtue and intelligence. And besides all this, I am afraid, Mamma, he has no real taste. Music seems scarcely to attract him, and though he admires Elinor's drawings very much, it is not the admiration of a person who can understand their worth. It is evident, in spite of his frequent attention to her while she draws, that in fact he knows nothing of the matter. He admires as a lover, not as a connoisseur."
Marianne Dashwood, SS

Slighting Someone

She was too much provoked and offended to have the power of directly saying any thing to the purpose. She could only give him a look; but it was such a look as she thought must restore him to his senses, and then left the sofa, removing to a seat by her sister, and giving her all her attention.
EM

Small Comfort

To be claimed as good, though in an improper style, is at least better than being rejected as no good at all.
PER

Small Talk

Mrs. A. sat darning a pair of stockings the whole of my visit. But do not mention this at home, lest a warning should act as an example. We afterwards walked together for an hour on the Cobb; she is very conversable in a common way; I do not perceive wit or genius, but she has sense and some degree of taste, and her manners are very engaging. She seems to like people rather too easily.
JAL

She was a great talker upon little matters, which exactly suited Mr. Woodhouse, full of trivial communications and harmless gossip.
EM

While Captains Wentworth and Harville led the talk on one side of the room, and by recurring to former days, supplied anecdotes in abundance to occupy and entertain the others, it fell to Anne's lot to be placed rather apart with Captain Benwick; and a very good impulse of her Nature obliged her to begin an acquaintance with him. He was shy, and disposed to abstraction; but the engaging mildness of her countenance, and gentleness of her manners, soon had their effect; and Anne was well repaid the first trouble of exertion.
PER

After a pause of some minutes, she addressed him a second time with: "It is *your* turn to say something now, Mr. Darcy—

I talked about the dance, and *you* ought to make some kind of remark on the size of the room, or the number of couples."

He smiled, and assured her that whatever she wished him to say should be said. "Very well.—That reply will do for the present.—Perhaps by and by I may observe that private balls are much pleasanter than public ones.—But *now* we may be silent."

"Do you talk by rule then, while you are dancing?"

"Sometimes. One must speak a little, you know. It would look odd to be entirely silent for half an hour together, and yet for the advantage of *some*, conversation ought to be so arranged as that they may have the trouble of saying as little as possible."

Elizabeth Bennet, Fitzwilliam Darcy, PP

Snobbery

She found him very capable of being a pleasant companion, and only prevented from being so always, by too great an aptitude to fancy himself as much superior to people in general.

SS

They were in fact very fine ladies, not deficient in good humour when they were pleased, nor in the power of being agreeable where they chose it; but proud and conceited. They were rather handsome, had been educated in one of the first private seminaries in town, had a fortune of twenty thousand pounds, were in the habit of spending more than they ought, and of associating with people of rank; and were therefore in every respect entitled to think well of themselves, and meanly of others.

PP

He was looked at with great admiration for about half the evening, till his manners gave a disgust which turned the

tide of his popularity; for he was discovered to be proud, to be above his company, and above being pleased; and not all his large estate in Derbyshire could then save him from having a most forbidding, disagreeable countenance, and being unworthy to be compared with his friend.
PP

"Could you expect me to rejoice in the inferiority of your connections? To congratulate myself on the hope of relations, whose condition in life is so decidedly beneath my own?"
Fitzwilliam Darcy, PP

"Well, it is the oddest thing to me, that a man should use such a pretty girl so ill! But when there is plenty of money on one side, and next to none on the other, Lord bless you! they care no more about such things!"
Mrs. Jennings, SS

"I would advise you merely to put on whatever of your clothes is superior to the rest, there is no occasion for any thing more. Lady Catherine will not think the worse of you for being simply dressed. She likes to have the distinction of rank preserved."
Mr. Collins, PP

Social Obligation

"My cousin Anne shakes her head. She is not satisfied. She is fastidious. My dear cousin . . . you have a better right to be fastidious than almost any other woman I know; but will it answer? Will it make you happy? Will it not be wiser to accept the society of those good ladies in Laura Place, and enjoy all the advantages of the connexion as far as possible?"
Mr. Elliot, PER

"My dear Emma," said he, moving from his chair into one close by her, "you are not going to tell me, I hope, that you had not a pleasant evening."

"Oh! no; I was pleased with my own perseverance in asking questions; and amused to think how little information I obtained."

George Knightley, Emma Woodhouse, EM

Social Pressure

"It is not that I am afraid of learning by heart," said Fanny, shocked to find herself at that moment the only speaker in the room, and to feel that almost every eye was upon her; "but I really cannot act."

"Yes, yes, you can act well enough for *us*. Learn your part, and we will teach you all the rest. You have only two scenes, and as I shall be Cottager, I'll put you in and push you about, and you will do it very well, I'll answer for it."

Fanny Price, Tom Bertram, MP

Social Rank

Anne was ashamed. Had Lady Dalrymple and her daughter even been very agreeable, she would still have been ashamed of the agitation they created, but they were nothing. There was no superiority of manner, accomplishment, or understanding. Lady Dalrymple had acquired the Name of "a charming woman," because she had a smile and a civil answer for everybody. Miss Carteret, with still less to say, was so plain and so awkward, that she would never have been tolerated in Camden Place but for her birth.

PER

She had a cultivated mind, and was, generally speaking, rational and consistent; but she had prejudices on the side of

ancestry; she had a value for rank and consequence, which blinded her a little to the faults of those who possessed them.
PER

"The nonsense and folly of people's stepping out of their rank and trying to appear above themselves, makes me think it right to give *you* a hint, Fanny, now that you are going into company without any of us; and I do beseech and entreat you not to be putting yourself forward, and talking and giving your opinion as if you were one of your cousins—as if you were dear Mrs. Rushworth or Julia. *That* will never do, believe me. Remember, wherever you are, you must be the lowest and last."
Mrs. Norris, MP

Delightful, charming, superior, first circles, spheres, lines, ranks, every thing. . . .
EM

Her daughter enjoyed a most uncommon degree of popularity for a woman neither young, handsome, rich, nor married. Miss Bates stood in the very worst predicament in the world for having much of the public favour; and she had no intellectual superiority to make atonement to herself, or frighten those who might hate her into outward respect.
EM

Solidity

Mrs. Croft, though neither tall nor fat, had a squareness, uprightness, and vigour of form, which gave importance to her person. She had bright dark eyes, good teeth, and altogether an agreeable face; though her reddened and weather-beaten complexion, the consequence of her having been almost as much at sea as her husband, made her seem to have lived

some years longer in the world than her real eight-and-thirty. Her manners were open, easy, and decided, like one who had no distrust of herself, and no doubts of what to do; without any approach to coarseness, however, or any want of good humour.
PER

Solitude and Its Pleasures

In such moments of precious, invaluable misery, she rejoiced in tears of agony to be at Cleveland; and as she returned by a different circuit to the house, feeling all the happy privilege of country liberty, of wandering from place to place in free and luxurious solitude, she resolved to spend almost every hour of every day while she remained with the Palmers, in the indulgence of such solitary rambles.
SS

Soul Mates

There are such beings in the world—perhaps one in a thousand—as the creature you and I should think perfection; where grace and spirit are united to worth, where the manners are equal to the heart and understanding; but such a person may not come in your way, or, if he does, he may not be the eldest son of a man of fortune, the near relation of your particular friend, and belonging to your own county.
JAL

Spoiled Nature

While well, and happy, and properly attended to, she had great good humour and excellent spirits; but any indisposi-

tion sunk her completely. She had no resources for solitude; and inheriting a considerable share of the Elliot self-importance, was very prone to add to every other distress that of fancying herself neglected and ill-used.
PER

Staying Single

She had the remembrance of all this, she had the consciousness of being nine-and-twenty to give her some regrets and some apprehensions; she was fully satisfied of being still quite as handsome as ever, but she felt her approach to the years of danger, and would have rejoiced to be certain of being properly solicited by baronet-blood within the next twelvemonth or two. Then might she again take up the book of books with as much enjoyment as in her early youth, but now she liked it not. Always to be presented with the date of her own birth and see no marriage follow but that of a youngest sister, made the book an evil; and more than once, when her father had left it open on the table near her, had she closed it, with averted eyes, and pushed it away.
PER

Sticky Situations

It was a very awkward moment; and the countenance of each shewed that it was so. They all looked exceedingly foolish; and Edward seemed to have as great an inclination to walk out of the room again, as to advance farther into it. The very circumstance, in its unpleasantest form, which they would each have been most anxious to avoid, had fallen on them.
SS

Stupidity

The indignities of stupidity, and the disappointments of selfish passion, can excite little pity.
MP

Surprises

"Surprises are foolish things. The pleasure is not enhanced, and the inconvenience is often considerable."
George Knightley, EM

Teasing

"Oh! shocking!" cried Miss Bingley, "I never heard any thing so abominable. How shall we punish him for such a speech?"

"Nothing so easy, if you have but the inclination," said Elizabeth."We can all plague and punish one another. Teaze him—laugh at him.—Intimate as you are, you must know how it is to be done."
Caroline Bingley, Elizabeth Bennet, PP

Temperament

"Though I would not say it to any body else, she has no more heart than a stone to people in general; and the devil of a temper."
Mr. Weston, EM

"Mr. Weston is rather an easy, cheerful-tempered man, than a man of strong feelings; he takes things as he finds them, and makes enjoyment of them somehow or other, depend-

ing, I suspect, much more upon what is called society for his comforts, that is, upon the power of eating and drinking, and playing whist with his neighbours five times a week, than upon family affection, or any thing that home affords."
John Knightley, EM

He was not an ill-tempered man, not so often unreasonably cross as to deserve such a reproach; but his temper was not his great perfection.
EM

Elizabeth was excessively disappointed; she had set her heart on seeing the Lakes . . . But it was her business to be satisfied—and certainly her temper to be happy, and all was soon right again.
PP

The simplicity and cheerfulness of her Nature, her contented and grateful spirit, were a recommendation to every body, and a mine of felicity to herself.
EM

A submissive spirit might be patient, a strong understanding would supply resolution, but here was something more; here was that elasticity of mind, that disposition to be comforted, that power of turning readily from evil to good, and of finding employment which carried her out of herself, which was from Nature alone. It was the choicest gift of heaven.
PER

Tenants

Mr. Shepherd was eloquent on the subject; pointing out all the circumstances of the Admiral's family, which made him

peculiarly desirable as a tenant. He was a married man, and without children; the very state to be wished for. A house was never taken good care of, Mr. Shepherd observed, without a lady: he did not know, whether furniture might not be in danger of suffering as much where there was no lady, as where there were many children. A lady, without a family, was the very best preserver of furniture in the world.
PER

Throwing Away One's Life

Anne Elliot, with all her claims of birth, beauty, and mind, to throw herself away at nineteen; involve herself at nineteen in an engagement with a young man, who had nothing but himself to recommend him, and no hopes of attaining affluence, but in the chances of a most uncertain profession, and no connexions to secure even his farther rise in the profession, would be, indeed, a throwing away, which she grieved to think of!
PER

Towns

"One has no great hopes from Birmingham. I always say there is something direful in the sound."
Mrs. Elton, EM

Travel and Sorrow

In this unceasing recurrence of doubts and inquiries . . . her journey advanced much faster than she looked for. The pressing anxieties of thought, which prevented her from noticing anything before her, when once beyond the neighbourhood of Woodston, saved her at the same time from

watching her progress; and though no object on the road could engage a moment's attention, she found no stage of it tedious. From this, she was preserved too by another cause, by feeling no eagerness for her journey's conclusion.
NA

Triteness

"Admiration of landscape scenery is become a mere jargon. Every body pretends to feel and tries to describe with the taste and elegance of him who first defined what picturesque beauty was. I detest jargon of every kind, and sometimes I have kept my feelings to myself, because I could find no language to describe them in but what was worn and hackneyed out of all sense and meaning."
Marianne Dashwood, SS

True Happiness

She might have been absolutely rich and perfectly healthy, and yet be happy. Her spring of felicity was in the glow of her spirits, as her friend Anne's was in the warmth of her heart.
PER

Unaffectedness

The Miss Dashwoods were young, pretty, and unaffected. It was enough to secure his good opinion; for to be unaffected was all that a pretty girl could want to make her mind as captivating as her person.
SS

Uncles

You must not be tired of reading the word *uncle*, for I have not done with it.
JAL

"If they had uncles enough to fill ALL Cheapside," cried Bingley, "it would not make them one jot less agreeable."
    "But it must very materially lessen their chance of marrying men of any consideration in the world," replied Darcy.
Charles Bingley, Fitzwilliam Darcy, PP

Understanding

Lady Middleton was equally pleased with Mrs. Dashwood. There was a kind of cold hearted selfishness on both sides, which mutually attracted them; and they sympathised with each other in an insipid propriety of demeanor, and a general want of understanding.
SS

Unhappy Engagement

Elinor sat down to the card table with the melancholy Persuasion that Edward was not only without affection for the person who was to be his wife; but that he had not even the chance of being tolerably happy in marriage, which sincere affection on HER side would have given, for self-interest alone could induce a woman to keep a man to an engagement, of which she seemed so thoroughly aware that he was weary.
SS

Unhappy Marriage

His temper might perhaps be a little soured by finding, like many others of his sex, that through some unaccountable bias in favour of beauty, he was the husband of a very silly woman,—but she knew that this kind of blunder was too common for any sensible man to be lastingly hurt by it.
SS

Unrequited Love

You know how I have loved you; you can intimately judge of my present feelings; but I am not so weak as to find indulgence in describing them to a woman who will glory in having excited their anguish, but whose affection they have never been able to gain.
LS

Unwanted Affection

"Can it be possible for this man to be beginning to transfer his affections from Harriet to me?—Absurd and insufferable!"
Emma Woodhouse, EM

Unwise Marriage

Poor Manwaring gives me such histories of his wife's jealousy. Silly Woman, to expect constancy from so charming a Man! but she always was silly—intolerably so in marrying him at all. She the Heiress of a large Fortune, he without a shilling! *One* title, I know, she might have had, besides Bar-

onets. Her folly in forming the connection was so great that tho' Mr. Johnson was her Guardian, & I do not in general share his feelings, I never can forgive her.
LS

Usefulness

To be claimed as a good, though in an improper style, is at least better than being rejected as no good at all; and Anne, glad to be thought of some use, glad to have anything marked out as a duty, and certainly not sorry to have the scene of it in the country, and her own dear country, readily agreed to stay.
PER

Vanity

She was not much deceived as to her own skill either as an artist or a musician, but she was not unwilling to have others deceived, or sorry to know her reputation for accomplishment often higher than it deserved.
EM

She *was* looked at however, and with some admiration; for in her own hearing, two gentlemen pronounced her to be a pretty girl. Such words had their effect; she immediately thought the evening pleasanter than she had found it before—her humble vanity was contented—she felt more obliged to the two young men for this simple praise than a true quality heroine would have been for fifteen sonnets in celebration of her charms, and went to her chair in good humour with everybody, and perfectly satisfied with her share of public attention.
NA

To be in company, nicely dressed herself and seeing others nicely dressed, to sit and smile and look pretty, and say nothing, was enough for the happiness of the present hour.
EM

"Vanity working on a weak head, produces every sort of mischief. Nothing so easy as for a young lady to raise her expectations too high."
George Knightley, EM

It was a struggle between propriety and vanity; but vanity got the better, and then Elizabeth was happy again.
PER

Like half the rest of the world, if more than half there be that are clever and good, Marianne, with excellent abilities and an excellent disposition, was neither reasonable nor candid. She expected from other people the same opinions and feelings as her own, and she judged of their motives by the immediate effect of their actions on herself.
SS

Vanity and pride

"Vanity and pride are different things, though the words are often used synonymously. A person may be proud without being vain. Pride relates more to our opinion of ourselves, vanity to what we would have others think of us."
Mary Bennet, PP

"Vanity is a weakness indeed. But pride—where there is a real superiority of mind, pride will always be under good regulation."
Fitzwilliam Darcy, PP

"I have always seen a great similarity in the turn of our minds—We are each of an unsocial, taciturn disposition, unwilling to speak, unless we expect to say something that will amaze the whole room, and be handed down to posterity with all the eclat of a proverb."
Elizabeth Bennet, PP

Vexation

She saw decision in his looks, and her surprise and vexation required some minutes' silence to be settled into composure.
MP

Villains

Fanny and the two little girls . . . revelled last night in Don Juan, whom we left in hell at half-past eleven. . . . The girls . . . still prefer Don Juan; and I must say that I have seen nobody on the stage who has been a more interesting character than that compound of cruelty and lust.
JAL

Catherine, at any rate, heard enough to feel that in suspecting General Tilney of either murdering or shutting up his wife, she had scarcely sinned against his character, or magnified his cruelty.
NA

"Many have been the cares and vicissitudes of my past life, my beloved Ellinor, & the only consolation I feel for their bitterness is that on close examination of my conduct, I am convinced that I strictly deserved them. I murdered my fa-

ther at a very early period of my Life, I have since murdered my Mother, and I am now going to murder my Sister. I have changed my religion so often that at present I have no idea of any left. I have been a perjured witness at every public tryal for these last twelve years; and I have forged my own will. In short, there is scarcely a crime I have not committed."
JU

Virtue

"Unhappy as the event must be . . . we may draw from it this useful lesson: that loss of virtue in a female is irretrievable; that one false step involves her in endless ruin; that her reputation is no less brittle than it is beautiful; and that she cannot be too much guarded in her behaviour towards the undeserving of the other sex."
Mary Bennet, PP

Visits to Relatives

It was a delightful visit;—perfect, in being much too short.
EM

Vulgarity

Mrs. Jennings, Lady Middleton's mother, was a good-humoured, merry, fat, elderly woman, who talked a great deal, seemed very happy, and rather vulgar. She was full of jokes and laughter, and before dinner was over had said many witty things on the subject of lovers and husbands; hoped they had not left their hearts behind them in Sussex, and pretended to see them blush whether they did or not.
SS

Wallflowers

Our ball was rather more amusing than I expected . . . The melancholy part was, to see so many dozen young women standing by without partners, and each of them with two ugly naked shoulders! It was the same room in which we danced fifteen years ago! I thought it all over, and in spite of the shame of being so much older, felt with thankfulness that I was quite as happy now as then.
JAL

Weakness

She had no scruples which could stand many minutes against the earnest pressing of both the others.
EM

"It is the worst evil of too yielding and indecisive a character, that no influence over it can be depended on. You are never sure of a good impression being durable; everybody may sway it. Let those who would be happy be firm."
Frederick Wentworth, PER

"He may have as strong a sense of what would be right, as you can have, without being so equal, under particular circumstances, to act up to it."
Emma Woodhouse, EM

Wealth

"People who have extensive grounds themselves are always pleased with any thing in the same style." Emma doubted the truth of this sentiment. She had a great idea that people who had extensive grounds themselves cared very little for the extensive grounds of any body else.
Mrs. Elton, EM

We found only Mrs. Lance at home, and whether she boasts any offspring besides a grand pianoforte did not appear. . . . They will not come often, I dare say. They live in a handsome style and are rich, and she seemed to like to be rich, and we gave her to understand that we were far from being so; she will soon feel therefore that we are not worth her acquaintance.
JAL

"Be honest and poor, by all means—but I shall not envy you; I do not much think I shall even respect you. I have a much greater respect for those that are honest and rich."
Mary Crawford, MP

Wealth and ambition

"I mean to be too rich to lament or to feel anything of the sort. A large income is the best recipe for happiness I ever heard of. It certainly may secure all the myrtle and turkey part of it."

"You intend to be very rich?" said Edmund, with a look which, to Fanny's eye, had a great deal of serious meaning.

"To be sure. Do not you? Do not we all?"
Mary Crawford, Edmund Bertram, MP

Wealth and appearance

Mr. Darcy soon drew the attention of the room by his fine, tall person, handsome features, noble mien; and the report which was in general circulation within five minutes after his entrance, of his having ten thousand a year. The gentlemen pronounced him to be a fine figure of a man, the ladies declared he was much handsomer than Mr. Bingley.
PP

Wealth and happiness

What Edward had done to forfeit the right of eldest son, might have puzzled many people to find out; and what Robert had done to succeed to it, might have puzzled them still more. It was an arrangement, however, justified in its effects, if not in its cause; for nothing ever appeared in Robert's style of living or of talking to give a suspicion of his regretting the extent of his income, as either leaving his brother too little, or bringing himself too much;—and if Edward might be judged from the ready discharge of his duties in every particular, from an increasing attachment to his wife and his home, and from the regular cheerfulness of his spirits, he might be supposed no less contented with his lot, no less free from every wish of an exchange.
SS

Wealth and its effects

I sent my answer . . . which I wrote without much effort, for I was rich, and the rich are always respectable, whatever be their style of writing.
JAL

"You are very fond of bending little minds; but where little minds belong to rich people in authority, I think they have a knack of swelling out, till they are quite as unmanageable as great ones."
Emma Woodhouse, EM

Weather

Here is a day for you! Did Bath or Ibthorp ever see a finer 8th of April? It is March and April together; the glare of the

one and the warmth of the other. We do nothing but walk about.
JAL

It is really too bad, and has been too bad for a long time, much worse than any one *can* bear, and I begin to think it will never be fine again. This is a *finesse* of mine, for I have often observed that if one writes about the weather, it is generally completely changed before the letter is read.
JAL

We have been exceedingly busy ever since you went away. In the first place we have had to rejoice two or three times every day at your having such very delightful weather for the whole of your journey.
JAL

How do you like this cold weather? I hope you have all been earnestly praying for it as a salutary relief from the dreadful mild and unhealthy season preceding it, fancying yourself half putrified from the want of it, and that now you all draw into the fire, complain that you never felt such bitterness of cold before, that you are half starved, quite frozen, and wish the mild weather back again with all your hearts.
JAL

I am sorry my mother has been suffering, and am afraid this exquisite weather is too good to agree with her. I enjoy it all over me, from top to toe, from right to left, longitudinally, perpendicularly, diagonally; and I cannot but selfishly hope we are to have it last till Christmas—nice, unwholesome, unseasonable, relaxing, close, muggy weather.
JAL

Rain

"How horrid all this is!" said he. "Such weather makes every thing and every body disgusting. Dullness is as much produced within doors as without, by rain. It makes one detest all one's acquaintance. What the devil does Sir John mean by not having a billiard room in his house? How few people know what comfort is! Sir John is as stupid as the weather."
Mr. Palmer, SS

How lucky we were in our weather yesterday! This wet morning makes one more sensible of it. We had no rain of any consequence. The head of the curricle was put half up three or four times, but our share of the showers was very trifling, though they seemed to be heavy all round us, when we were on the Hog's-back, and I fancied it might then be raining so hard at Chawton as to make you feel for us much more than we deserved.
JAL

Weddings

The wedding took place; the bride and bridegroom set off for Kent from the church door, and every body had as much to say or to hear on the subject as usual.
PP

"Well," said Emma, willing to let it pass—"you want to hear about the wedding; and I shall be happy to tell you, for we all behaved charmingly. Every body was punctual, every body in their best looks: not a tear, and hardly a long face to be seen."
Emma Woodhouse, EM

It was a very proper wedding. The bride was elegantly dressed; the two bridesmaids were duly inferior; her father gave her away; her mother stood with salts in her hand, expecting to be agitated; her aunt tried to cry; and the service was impressively read by Dr. Grant. Nothing could be objected to when it came under the discussion of the neighbourhood, except that the carriage which conveyed the bride and bridegroom and Julia from the church-door to Sotherton, was the same chaise which Mr. Rushworth had used for a twelvemonth before. In everything else the etiquette of the day might stand the strictest investigation.
MP

Miss Bigg . . . writes me word that Miss Blachford is married. But I have never seen it in the Paper. And one may be as well be single, if the Wedding is not to be in print.
JAL

Wickedness

What wicked people dyers are. They begin with dipping their own souls in scarlet sin.
JAL

Widows

That Lady Russell, of steady age and character, and extremely well provided for, should have no thought of a second marriage, needs no apology to the public, which is rather apt to be unreasonably discontented when a woman does marry again, than when she does not; but Sir Walter's continuing in singleness requires explanation.
PER

Mrs. John Lyford is so much pleased with the state of widowhood as to be going to put in for being a widow again; she is to marry a Mr. Fendall.
JAL

Willfulness

She left her seat, she would go; one half of her should not be always so much wiser than the other half, or always suspecting the other of being worse than it was.
PER

You found my letter at Andover, I hope, yesterday, and have now for many hours been satisfied that your kind anxiety on my behalf was as much thrown away as kind anxiety usually is.
JAL

Wit and Lying

Catherine listened with astonishment; she knew not how to reconcile two such very different accounts of the same thing; for she had not been brought up to understand the propensities of a rattle, nor to know to how many idle assertions and impudent falsehoods the excess of vanity will lead. Her own family were plain, matter-of-fact people who seldom aimed at wit of any kind; her father, at the utmost, being contented with a pun, and her mother with a proverb; they were not in the habit therefore of telling lies to increase their importance, or of asserting at one moment what they would contradict the next.
NA

Women

It is only by seeing women in their own homes, among their own set, just as they always are, that you can form any just judgment. Short of that, it is all guess and luck.
EM

Where people wish to attach, they should always be ignorant. To come with a well-informed mind is to come with an inability of administering to the vanity of others, which a sensible person would always wish to avoid. A woman especially, if she have the misfortune of knowing anything, should conceal it as well as she can.
NA

Women and admiration

"We must not be so ready to fancy ourselves intentionally injured. We must not expect a lively young man to be always so guarded and circumspect. It is very often nothing but our own vanity that deceives us. Women fancy admiration means more than it does."
Jane Bennet, PP

Women and men

"Miss Morland, no one can think more highly of the understanding of women than I do. In my opinion, Nature has given them so much that they never find it necessary to use more than half."
Henry Tilney, NA

Women and reckoning

"I am really not tired, which I almost wonder at; for we must have walked at least a mile in this wood. Do not you think we have?"

"Not half a mile," was his sturdy answer; for he was not yet so much in love as to measure distance, or reckon time, with feminine lawlessness.

Mary Crawford, Edmund Bertram, MP

Women and time

"We have been exactly a quarter of an hour here," said Edmund, taking out his watch. "Do you think we are walking four miles an hour?"

"Oh! do not attack me with your watch. A watch is always too fast or too slow. I cannot be dictated to by a watch."

Edmund Bertram, Mary Crawford, MP

Words

I called yesterday morning [—] ought it not in strict propriety to be termed yester-morning?

JAL

Work and Pleasure

"Business, you know, may bring money, but friendship hardly ever does."

John Knightley, EM

Worthiness

Nobody minds having what is too good for them.
MP

Writing

"It is one thing," said she, presently—her cheeks in a glow—
"to have very good sense in a common way, like every body
else, and if there is any thing to say, to sit down and write a
letter, and say just what you must, in a short way; and another, to write verses and charades like this."
Harriet Smith, EM

Expect a most agreeable letter, for not being overburdened
with subject having nothing at all to say, I shall have no
check to my genius from beginning to end.
JAL

Let other pens dwell on guilt and misery. I quit such odious
subjects as soon as I can.
MP

I could no more write a [historical] romance than an epic
poem. I could not sit seriously down to write a serious romance under any other motive than to save my life; and if it
were indispensable for me to keep it up and never relax into
laughing at myself or other people, I am sure I should be
hung before I had finished the first chapter.
JAL

I often wonder how you can find time for what you do, in
addition to the care of the house; and how good Mrs. West
could have written such books and collected so many hard
works, with all her family cares, is still more a matter of as-

tonishment! Composition seems to me impossible with a headfull of joints of mutton and doses of rhubarb.
JAL

Writing a novel

[On *Pride and Prejudice:*] Upon the whole, however, I am quite vain enough and well satisfied enough. The work is rather too light, and bright, and sparkling; it wants shade; it wants to be stretched out here and there with a long chapter of sense, if it could be had; if not, of solemn specious nonsense, about something unconnected with the story; an essay on writing, a critique on Walter Scott, or the history of Buonaparté, or anything that would form a contrast, and bring the reader with increased delight to the playfulness and epigrammatism of the general style.
JAL

Yes and No

The issue of all depended on one question. Did she love him well enough to forego what had used to be essential points? Did she love him well enough to make them no longer essential? And this question, which he was continually repeating to himself, though oftenest answered with a "Yes," had sometimes its "No."
MP

Young Ladies

"Young ladies are delicate plants. They should take care of their health and their complexion."
Mr. Woodhouse, EM

Young Love

His heart was now open to Elinor, all its weaknesses, all its errors confessed, and his first boyish attachment to Lucy treated with all the philosophic dignity of twenty-four.
SS

Young Men

". . . not like the wild young men nowadays, who think of nothing but themselves."
Mrs. Reynolds, PP

"They are young in the ways of the world, and not yet open to the mortifying conviction that handsome young men must have something to live on as well as the plain."
Elizabeth Bennet, PP

"He is just what a young man ought to be," said she, "sensible, good humoured, lively."

"He is also handsome," replied Elizabeth, "which a young man ought likewise to be, if he possibly can. His character is thereby complete."
Jane Bennet, Elizabeth Bennet, PP

Youth

Emma Woodhouse, . . . handsome, clever, and rich, with a comfortable home and happy disposition, seemed to unite some of the best blessings of existence; and had lived nearly twenty-one years in the world with very little to distress or vex her.
EM

Youthful Folly

". . . and yet there is something so amiable in the prejudices of a young mind, that one is sorry to see them give way to the reception of more general opinions."

"I cannot agree with you there," said Elinor. "There are inconveniences attending such feelings as Marianne's, which all the charms of enthusiasm and ignorance of the world cannot atone for."

Colonel Brandon, Elinor Dashwood, SS

BIBLIOGRAPHY

Works by Jane Austen

Sense and Sensibility (1811)

Pride and Prejudice (1813)

Mansfield Park (1814)

Emma (1816)

Northanger Abbey (1818, published posthumously)

Persuasion (1818, published posthumously)

Sanditon (unfinished, fragmentary draft, published posthumously)

Lady Susan (juvenilia, published posthumously)

Love and Friendship (juvenilia, published posthumously)

The Watsons (juvenilia, published posthumously)

The History of England: From the Reign of Henry the 4th to the Death of Charles the 1st (juvenilia, published posthumously)

Penguin Classics, a division of Penguin Books, London, has published updated and annotated editions of all of Jane Austen's works, including a volume of her juvenilia.

Selected Works for Further Reading

Abbott, Rob, et al. *Jane Austen: A Beginner's Guide*, Hodder & Stoughton (2002).

Austen, Jane. *The Complete Novels*, Grammercy (1994).

Austen, Jane, and Margaret Drabble, ed. *Lady Susan: The Watsons: Sanditon,* Penguin English Library, Viking Press (1975).

Austen-Leigh, James Edward. *A Memoir of Jane Austen*, Richard Bentley (1870).

Austen-Leigh, William, and Richard Arthur. *Jane Austen, Her Life and Letters: A Family Record*, Reprint Services Corp. (1913).

Austen-Leigh, William, and Richard Arthur; revised and enlarged by Deirdre Le Faye. *Jane Austen: A Family Record*, The British Library (1989).

Bloom, Harold, ed. *Modern Critical Views, Jane Austen*, Chelsea House Publishers (1986).

Bradbrook, F. W. *Jane Austen and Her Predecessors*, Cambridge University Press (1966).

Burrows, John. *Computation into Criticism: A Study of Jane Austen's Novels, and an Experiment in Method*, Oxford University Press (1987).

Butler, Marilyn. *Jane Austen and the War of Ideas*, Clarendon Press (1993).

Byatt, A. S., et al. *Imagining Characters: Conversations About Women Writers: Jane Austen, Charlotte Brontë, George Eliot, Willa Cather, Iris Murdoch, and Toni Morrison*, Vintage Books (1997).

Cecil, David. *Portrait of Jane Austen*, Penguin (1978).

Craik, W. A. *Jane Austen: The Six Novels*, Methuen (1965).

————. *Jane Austen in Her Time*, Nelson (1969).

Doody, Margaret Anne, and Douglas Murray, eds. *Catharine and Other Writings*, Oxford University Press (1998).

Foreman, Amanda. *Georgiana: Duchess of Devonshire*, Modern Library (2001).

Gillie, Christopher. *A Preface to Jane Austen*, Longman (2001).

Greefield, Troost, et al., eds. *Jane Austen in Hollywood*, The University Press of Kentucky (1998).

Grey, J. David, ed.; A. Walton Litz and Brian Southam, consulting eds. *The Jane Austen Companion* (with *A Dictionary of Jane Austen's Life and Works* by H. Abigail Bok), Macmillan (1986).

————, ed. *Jane Austen's Beginnings: The Juvenilia and Lady Susan*, UMI Research Press (1989).

Halperin, John. *The Life of Jane Austen*, Johns Hopkins University Press (1984).

Hardwick, Michael. *A Guide to Jane Austen*, Charles Scribner's Sons (1973).

Hawkridge, Audrey. *Jane and Her Gentlemen: Jane Austen and the Men in Her Life and Novels*, Peter Owen Ltd. (2001).

Heath, William. *Discussions of Jane Austen*, D. C. Heath (1961).

Honan, Park. *Jane Austen: Her Life*, Weidenfeld (1987).

Hughes-Hallett, Penelope. *The Illustrated Letters of Jane Austen*, Clarkson Potter/Publishers (1991).

Jenkins, Elizabeth. *Jane Austen: A Biography*, Gollancz (1938).

Johnson, Claudia. *Jane Austen: Women, Politics, and the Novel*, University of Chicago Press (1988).

Kirkham, Margaret. *Jane Austen, Feminism and Fiction*, Harvester Press/Barnes & Noble (1983).

Lane, Maggie. *Jane Austen's World, The Life and Times of England's Most Popular Author*, Adams Media Corporation (1997).

———. *Jane Austen's Family*, Robert Hale Ltd. (2001).

Lascelles, Mary. *Jane Austen and Her Art*, Oxford University Press (1939/1954).

Laski, Marghanita. *Jane Austen and Her World*, Viking (1969).

Leavis, F. R. *The Great Tradition*, Chatto and Windus (1947).

Le Faye, Deirdre, ed. *Jane Austen's Letters*, 3d ed., Oxford University Press (1995). [Earlier editions edited by Chapman.]

———. *Jane Austen's Outlandish Cousin: The Life and Letters of Eliza De Feuillide*, British Library Publications (2002).

Lynch, Deidre, ed. *Janeites*, Princeton University Press (2000).

Mudrick, Marvin. *Jane Austen: Irony as Defense and Discovery*, University of California Press (1952).

Myer, Valerie Grosvenor. *Jane Austen: Obstinate Heart*, Arcade Publishing (1997).

Nokes, David. *Jane Austen: A Life*, Farrar Straus & Giroux (1997).

Nugent, Christopher, et al. *Jane Austen: Illusion and Reality*, Boydell & Brewer (1999).

Pool, Daniel. *What Jane Austen Ate and Charles Dickens Knew: From Fox Hunting to Whist—The Facts of Daily Life in Nineteenth-Century England*, Touchstone Books (1994).

Porter, Roy. *English Society in the Eighteenth Century (Penguin Social History of Britain)*, Penguin U.S.A. (1990).

Nicolson, Nigel. *The World of Jane Austen*, Weidenfield and Nicolson (1991).

Saul, David. *Prince of Pleasure: The Prince of Wales and the Making of the Regency*, Grove Press (2000).

Shields, Carol. *Jane Austen (Penguin Lives)*, Viking Press (2001).

Southam, B. C. *Jane Austen's Literature Manuscripts: A Study of the Novelist's Development Through the Surviving Papers*, Continuum (2002).

———. *Jane Austen: The Critical Heritage*, Routledge & K. Paul (1968); vol. 2 *1870–1940* (1987).

———, ed. *Jane Austen: Sense and Sensibility, Pride and Prejudice, and Mansfield Park: A Casebook*, Macmillan (1976).

———, ed. *Northanger Abbey and Persuasion: A Casebook*, Macmillan (1976).

———. *Jane Austen and the Navy*, Hambledon Press (2001).

Tanner, Tony. *Jane Austen*, Macmillan (1986).

Tomalin, Claire. *Jane Austen: A Life*, Alfred A. Knopf (1997).

Tucker, George Holbert. *Jane Austen the Woman: Some Biographical Insights*, St. Martin's Press (1994).

Vickery, Amanda. *The Gentleman's Daughter; Lives in Georgian England*, Yale University Press (1998).

Waldron, Mary. *Jane Austen and the Fiction of Her Time*, Cambridge University Press (1999).

Watkins, Susan, et al. *Jane Austen: In Style*, Thames & Hudson (1996).

Weldon, Fay. *Letters to Alice on First Reading Jane Austen*, Michael Joseph (1984).

Wilkes, Brian. *Jane Austen*, Hammond (1978).

Woolf, Virginia. "Jane Austen at Sixty," *Nation*, vol. XXXIV (15 December 1923), p. 433.

ACKNOWLEDGMENTS

Special thanks to acquisitions editor Margaret Wolf for her encouragement, patience, and wonderful editing, and to Joan Matthews for copyediting the manuscript. Undying gratitude to Francine Hornberger and Christine Marie, without their editorial skills and timely assistance this book would never have been finished. Heartfelt thanks to Jay, for always cooking and never complaining, to Liz, for her support, optimism, and babysitting, and to Isabelle, just for being wonderful.

ABOUT THE EDITOR

Shawna Mullen is a writer and editor. She lives in Beverly Farms, Massachusetts, with her husband and daughter. She would most like to resemble Elizabeth Bennet from *Pride and Prejudice*, but fears she is more like Lydia—"a flirt in the worst and meanest degree of flirtation. . . . Vain, ignorant, idle, and absolutely uncontrolled!"